Policing Matters

Study Skills for Policing Students

Policing Matters

Study Skills for Policing Students

Richard Malthouse
Jodi Roffey-Barentsen

Series editors
P A J Waddington
Martin Wright

British Library Cataloguing in Publication Data
A CIP record for this book is available from the British Library.

ISBN: 978 1 84445 352 8

This book is also available in the following ebook formats:

Adobe ebook   ISBN: 978 1 84445 661 1
ePub ebook   ISBN: 978 1 84445 660 4
Kindle   ISBN: 978 1 84445 971 1

The rights of Richard Malthouse and Jodi Roffey-Barentsen to be identified as the Authors of this work have been asserted by them in accordance with the Copyright, Design and Patents Act 1988.

Cover design by Toucan Graphic Design Ltd
Text design by Code 5 Design Associates
Project management by Diana Chambers
Typeset by Kelly Winter
Printed and bound in Great Britain by TJ International, Padstow, Cornwall

Learning Matters Ltd
33 Southernhay East
Exeter EX1 1NX
Tel: 01392 215560
info@learningmatters.co.uk
www.learningmatters.co.uk

All weblinks and web addresses in the book have been carefully checked prior to publication, but for up-to-date information please visit the Learning Matters website, www.learningmatters.co.uk.

The authors would like to thank Jennifer Clark for her assistance with this book.

Contents

1 Getting started

CHAPTER OBJECTIVES

By the end of this chapter you will be able to:

- state the causes of procrastination;
- identify the specific study skills that require your attention;
- recognise the benefits of intrinsic motivation;
- apply the principles of time/activity management;
- employ the use of an activity schedule;
- state the importance of maintaining concentration;
- split your work into manageable chunks;
- maintain a positive attitude towards study;
- recognise the influence of personal filters;
- state the five levels of competence;
- conduct reflective practice.

LINKS TO STANDARDS

This chapter provides opportunities for links with the following Skills for Justice, National Occupational Standards (NOS) for Policing and Law Enforcement 2008.

AB1.1 Communicate effectively with people.
AE1.1 Maintain and develop your own knowledge, skills and competence.
HA1 Manage your own resources.
HA2 Manage your own resources and professional development.

Links to NOS will be provided at the start of each chapter; however, it should be noted that the NOS are subject to review and it is recommended that you visit the Skills for Justice website to check the currency of all the NOS provided: www.skillsforjustice-nosfinder.com.

Introduction

This chapter offers guidance as you prepare for study. For some, study may be something that you have been doing for years and you are reading this book to glean any suggestions that may benefit future learning. Others may be returning to study following years of no study whatsoever and are reading this book to find out what study skills are all about. Whatever your reasons for reading this book, the fact that you are interested in improving your study skills means that your attitude towards your own study skills is commendable, and that you are exhibiting a healthy attitude towards your learning and, therefore, your future.

One lesson you may have found to be missing when you were at school was called 'How to Study'. It was just assumed that people knew how to study and were, therefore, given things to learn. Nothing could be further from the truth. People think they know how to study, but sometimes the strategies they employ can be very long-winded and consequently a waste of time. For example, have you ever tried to learn something by writing it out a hundred times? Did you actually learn the information, or did you just regurgitate it verbatim? Rather than write it out time and again, you could have spoken out loud, which is far quicker. Alternatively, you could have discussed your understanding of the topic with another person and then answered any questions they may have had. This is just one example of the many alternative ways there are to study. Remember – if you always do what you always did, you will always get what you always got.

Studying is a skill and all skills benefit from analysis and practice. Analysis means that we will be breaking the component parts of study down into manageable chunks, giving you the opportunity to consider each part critically. Having identified the various parts that constitute study, you can then begin to practise them. To assist you with this task, a short questionnaire has been designed (see the first 'Practical task' below), enabling you to identify which elements of study skills you should practise and their location within this book.

The aspects of study this chapter considers include the themes, 'Getting started' and 'Motivation', as for some these are easier said than done. Next, 'Time management' is examined and 'Activity scheduling' is described and demonstrated. 'Concentration' is considered and guidance is offered in relation to those occasions when you find your mind wandering. 'Chunking' study into manageable tasks is discussed and 'Attitude to study' is considered in terms of the advantages of displaying a positive attitude towards your study. The concept of 'Personal filters' is noted, giving you the opportunity to identify some of your unique characteristics. Your learning journey involves what are referred to as 'Steps of competence', and these are discussed to assist your understanding of your own progress. Lastly, the benefit of 'Reflective practice' is highlighted as a tool to assist your learning by questioning your assumptions and researching solutions. As with any book, you can read it from cover to cover or, if you are keen to manage your time effectively, concentrate on those topics that will benefit you the most.

Getting started

Sometimes the first step in any journey can be the most difficult. If you are inclined to procrastinate, you may find that there is always something else to do that is more enjoyable than the task you know you have to do. You may find yourself in a position where you have bought new pens, paper, folders and books, but still have not got around to actually doing any study. The reason for not starting a task differs from person to person but frequently the reasons can include:

- a lack of confidence;
- low self-esteem;
- stress;
- anxiety;
- fear of the unknown;
- not wanting to take responsibility;
- lack of self-belief;
- being too busy with other things.

People are motivated by many influences, but to generalise, they can be anywhere between two points:

Or more succinctly:

The task remains the same whether it is done now or later and, generally, it does not go away or become any easier the longer you choose to do something else. If you are the type of person who is full of good intentions that never quite come to fruition, now may be a good time to re-evaluate your past habits and change your behaviour. One reason why people do not get around to the task in hand is because it is seen to be too large and therefore too onerous.

Tracy (2004) considers the issue of procrastination and uses the analogy of the frog to describe that of starting a task. The rule is that the frog must be consumed at some stage during the day. Obviously, the concept of eating a frog is naturally unpleasant for most and he asks whether people would:

- eat it first thing to get it out of the way;
- procrastinate and eat it last thing; or
- eat it over the course of a day, little by little.

The concept of the frog is useful when you think about your own behaviour. For most, breaking a task down into manageable chunks is the preferred option. But how do you break down your tasks into manageable chunks? Take, for example, the task of improving your study skills. If you want to improve, it may be useful to analyse your ability and your behaviour. The following questions are designed to help you to do this.

PRACTICAL TASK

Indicate with a tick in the boxes below which best describes you.

Statement	Yes – does not require attention	Yes – but can be improved	No – needs to be addressed
1. I am motivated to study			
2. I persevere when it gets difficult			
3. I manage my time well between study and a social life			
4. I meet deadlines			
5. I never cram the work in the night before test or assignment deadlines			
6. I never study with the music or the television on			
7. When I study I do not become tired easily			
8. When I study I don't become bored or easily distracted			
9. In lessons I never doodle or find my mind wandering on to other things			
10. I am full of enthusiasm at the start of a course			
11. My enthusiasm for a task does not wane			
12. If I have a choice of doing anything, study comes first			
13. I like the subject matter and the tutor			
14. I reflect on my work			
15. When reading I never find that my eyes have been going over the words while I was thinking about other things			
16. When I get to the end of a chapter, I can remember what I have read			
17. I read competently up to Level 2 (GCSE)			
18. I read competently at Level 3 and above (A level to undergraduate)			
19. I take notes effectively in class			
20. I use mind/concept maps when taking notes			

Statement	Yes – does not require attention	Yes – but can be improved	No – needs to be addressed
21. I know how to structure an assignment			
22. I am confident in using English grammar and punctuation correctly			
23. I am confident about my writing skills, putting things in my own words			
24. I can cite and reference accurately			
25. I can compare and contrast other people's opinions			
26. I can evaluate other people's writing and form an argument			
27. I cooperate with others in a learning situation			
28. I am confident with my computer skills for study			
29. I feel confident in structuring a presentation			
30. I feel confident in delivering a presentation			
31. I am confident in memorising facts			
32. I know how to revise for an exam			
33. I prepare effectively for an exam			
34. I am confident in researching a topic using a range of sources (books, journals, internet)			
35. I am familiar with the research process			
36. I can organise the different chapters in a dissertation			

There is no chart to complete for the results of this task to tell you what type of person you are, as that is immaterial. You have simply identified the areas upon which you must concentrate. Table 1.1 indicates where in this book you can locate advice on your weaker areas.

Table 1.1 Where to find the topics you need

Statements	Topic	Addressed in chapter
1–2	Motivation	1
3–5	Time management	1
6–9	Concentration	1
10–13	Attitude	1
14	Reflective practice	1
15–18	Reading	2
19–20	Note-taking	2
21–24	Writing skills	3
25–26	Critical and analytical thinking skills	4
27	Collaborative learning	5
28	The use of ICT	6
29–30	Presentations	7
31–33	Exams	8
34–35	Research	9
36	Writing your dissertation	10

The choice is yours; you can either read this book from cover to cover, or read only the parts that you have identified as being relevant to your individual needs. Hopefully you can turn your frog into something more appetising.

REFLECTIVE TASK

Think about and list the behaviours that you feel are indicative of a negative attitude to study. Next do the same for a positive attitude to study. When you compare them what are the underlying characteristics?

It is likely that your lists in the above task will be underpinned by considerations of perceived ability and motivation. We like to do what we can do well, and that which we find difficult we are less inclined to engage in. If you have struggled with study, it is likely that you will not enjoy it. This book will guide you through the process of improving your study skills so that you can not only do the things you enjoy but can also embrace the things you do less well.

The individual topics are now considered under the relevant headings:

- motivation;
- time management;
- activity scheduling;
- concentration;
- chunking;
- attitude to study;

- personal filters;
- reflective practice.

Motivation

Ormrod (2008, p407) suggests that motivation is 'an internal state that arouses us to action, pushes us in particular directions, and keeps us engaged in certain activities'. Being motivated to do something is dependent upon the situation in which you find yourself. For example, if you have nowhere to live and you are hungry, you may not be motivated to study as other more pressing considerations may be occupying your time. However, most students are fortunate to have somewhere to live and plenty of food. What motivates them to study is a moot point. It is generally accepted that there are two forms of motivation: extrinsic and intrinsic. Extrinsic motivation can exist as a result of something outside an individual that compels them to a course of action. An example of this would be working in a horrible job to be rewarded by payment at the end of the week; the external motivation is the reward of money. Alternatively, a person may be paid little or nothing by working with the homeless or disabled. Their motivation is intrinsic as the work done rewards them in terms of the joy they get by helping others.

If a person studies because they have been tasked with an assignment in which they have no interest, the motivation is extrinsic, and it is less likely that the person will work hard at the task and in some cases may not complete it. If the person is intrinsically motivated to complete the task because they enjoy the subject, want to do well and achieve, they are more likely to engage fully and complete the task. It is by buying into a subject and applying yourself to your studies that you are likely to be motivated to achieve and do well. Motivation is a state of mind and is arguably something that can be changed, but the only person who can make this change is you. The following list of habits is designed to help you with your motivation.

Seven good habits of motivation

1. Identify a goal and put it in writing.

2. Set a start date and keep to it.

3. Set a completion date and keep to it.

4. Involve yourself with others who are motivated.

5. Don't be distracted.

6. If what you are doing is not working, do something else.

7. Reward yourself for achieving a goal.

Motivation is all about making the effort for you and believing in yourself. If you don't believe in yourself, who will? Study takes effort and you need to be motivated to make that effort. It's fine having a dream, but if you want to achieve your dream, the first thing you have to do is to wake up.

Time management

Arguably, the term 'time management', is a misnomer, as you can no more manage time than you can turn the tide or move the moon. What you can do though is identify what you do in the time available. What you are doing here, in fact, is better described as activity management.

Identifying how many hours there are in a day is a complete waste of time because, as you know, time has elastic qualities. Sometimes it goes very slowly and on other occasions it whips past you at the speed of light, normally when you are enjoying yourself.

What you need to do is take control of your activities and arrange them so that you can use your activities constructively. Cottrell (1999, p64) suggests that, 'As only part of your week and year will be formally timetabled, you will be responsible for organising most of your study time.' But we are creatures of habit and not all habits are good. It is a strange phenomenon that, if asked, we cannot state exactly how much of the day our activities take up. If you are employed, often a typical working day is about eight hours, and here the law of thirds comes into play: eight hours sleeping, eight hours at work and eight hours getting to and from work, doing jobs around the house, eating, watching the television, walking the dog, washing, ironing, etc. If you are a working part-time student the last third is even more hectic, while the character of a full-time student's day is completely different.

REFLECTIVE TASK

To find out how much time your activities take in a week, complete the matrix below.

Time/activity matrix

Activity	Hrs per day	Hrs per week	Total
How many hours a day do you typically spend washing and dressing, etc?			
How much time do you spend commuting to and from college/university? Include walking to the bus train. etc.			
How many hours a day do you spend preparing, eating and cleaning up after meals?			
How many hours do you spend each week doing other things, such as attending the gym, religious functions, sport, etc?			
How much time a day do you spend doing jobs?			
How much time a day do you spend playing computer games?			
How much time do you spend in class each week?			
How much time per week do you work at a job?			
How much time per week do you spend socialising with friends, going out, attending parties, etc?			
How much time per week do you spend watching the television/ DVDs or going to the cinema?			
Total			

There are 168 hours in a week; time for sleep of eight hours per day = 56. If you are getting less than eight hours' sleep, you will suffer and so will your study. So, 168 – 56 = 112.

Take from 112 the total identified in the above task. The figure remaining is the time you have left for study, as that has not been included yet.

By now you may have realised that, in order to study, you may need to rearrange the activities in your life.

Activity scheduling

In order to make space in your daily routine for study, you will be required to rearrange your daily routine. For some, this may be the first time that such an activity will be necessary. This is a good thing and will help prepare you for your time as a police officer when, on top of all your activities, you will also have shift work to consider.

As a student you will be expected to attend lessons and then study out of class time in preparation for an assignment or examination. If you want to be successful, it is imperative that you spend time studying and not doing things that will distract you from your goal. Many students discover that the full-time job of being a student is affected by the need to find a part-time job, while others may have family commitments to contend with. Because of these other factors making demands on your time, a coping strategy is required. This can be achieved by activity scheduling. It is recommended that you use a combination of long- and short-range activity schedules. The long-range schedule can be used to manage a semester, while the short-range schedule is suitable for a week. Exactly how you design the schedule is a matter for you. We recommend either using a table in a Word document or a form of spreadsheet. Remember, on the weekly schedule, rather than writing 'study' try to be specific – what exactly are you going to study ?

Consider which lessons you must prepare for and arrange your study methodically. There is little point in working hard, but missing deadlines, because you have been too busy doing something that does not need to be handed in until two weeks from now. Try not to be too rigid in your scheduling; new students fail to keep to a schedule not because they are organised but because they are too organised. If every hour and minute of the day is accounted for in your schedule, an uninvited guest can put your plans out. Once your schedule is out of sync, you will find it demoralising and from that time it is difficult to get back on track. Allowing for flexibility will ensure that you have extra capacity to accommodate unexpected events without them having a negative impact. Within the schedule, indicate what is non-negotiable, such as times of lessons, events, sleep and work. The study can then be woven around these.

The amount of time given to study depends on many things, for example whether you are a full- or part-time student, the number of hours you are expected to attend, your domestic situation, etc. What is almost certain is that you will have to re-evaluate the amount of time you study with a view to increasing that time.

It is good practice to get into a routine. Studying at the same time every day will assist in this. Doing this during the week at least will mean that you can follow a fixed schedule as far as possible. Some time that is easily wasted is situated in between your lessons. It is very important to socialise, but excessive socialising eats into your valuable study time. Following a lesson, go to the library or learning resource centre (LRC), where socialising is less easy, and make a start on any of the tasks that have been set during the day. There is no time like the present; in fact the present is all you will ever have, so make the most of it.

An example of activity scheduling is shown below:

Activity Schedule, Monday 22nd

	1	2		3	4		5	6		7
Time	09:00 09:45	09:45 10:30		10:50 11:35	11:35 12:20		13:20 14:05	14:05 14:50		15:10 16:00
Mon	SOCAP 2005 MA3	B R E A K		Library res'ch Essay 1.1	Use of force MA1	L U N C H	Tutorial 13:40– 14:00 J Oag MA14	First aid EB2	B R E A K	Giving evidence

	8	9	10	11	12	13	14	15
Time	16:00 17:00	17:00 18:00	18:00 19:00	19:00 20:00	20:00 21:00	21:00 22:00	22:00 23:00	24:00 08:00
Mon	Travel to home and eat	Essay 1.1 reading and planning	Essay 1.1 reading and planning	Break	Essay 1.2 first draft	Revision for test Thurs.	Revision for test Thurs. until 22.30	

The schedule should be flexible enough for change where necessary, but rigid enough for you to stick to. A plan such as this is important as it makes best use of your time.

Concentration

Selecting an appropriate place to study is important. If you share a house, studying with a laptop in the lounge with your friends may feel good, but the distractions will mean that you are unlikely to remain focused. You will benefit from reducing distractions such as noise, phone calls, texts, emails, children, relatives and relatives people in general. Most people end up studying in their own room or somewhere in their house away from the distraction of others. If you have a set routine, it is easier for other people in the house to appreciate that, at a certain time, they should not bother you as you are studying.

Alternatively, if the house is not appropriate there are places in college to study, for example the LRC or library.

When choosing a place to study you should aim to find a place that benefits from:

- few distractions;
- suitable ventilation;
- adequate lighting;
- a suitable chair;
- a desk that is large enough for you to spread out your study material.

If you have a place you associate just with study, you will find that this will make studying easier. In order to be able to concentrate, it will be necessary to take regular breaks. You know best how you feel as you work, but generally it is good practice to work for about 45 minutes to an hour and then take a ten-minute break.

If you find that your mind has wandered, you need to break away from that state. Get up and face away from your work, just for a moment. The physical effect should be enough to take you out of your daydream or musings. Another technique when reading is to slowly count to ten at the end of each page. For some, it keeps their minds focused on the meaning of the words, rather than allowing the eyes to move over the words but failing to make sense of their meaning.

Chunking

Your concentration will be further assisted if you have a specific goal or aim to work towards. This can be achieved by looking at the work and dividing it into manageable chunks. When you start, make the chunks small and relatively easy, as this way you will achieve your goals. As you practise this you will be better able to choose the appropriate size of the chunks to fit into your allocated time.

Don't be tempted to work flat out until you cannot go on. This is counter-productive as eventually you will exhaust yourself. Just a few breaks make all the difference. Some find goal sheets support study: you write on a piece of paper the task and the time you expect to finish; do this on every occasion so that you can see a record of your progress. As you do this, try to include a little more work within the time you have given yourself; this will make your study more efficient as you practise. Leaving work incomplete should be avoided. If you have found that a little more time is required, consider it as an extra chunk of work. Take a break and then get back to the task. The reason for this is that, for some, the state of mind associated with an incomplete task means that all they think about is that task and not the material that has been successfully completed. Learning does not just take place in the classroom or during times of study; insights can be found at any time during periods of reflection.

Attitude to study

A positive attitude towards your learning experience can carry you through the hardest times. There are some very talented and bright students who will never achieve academically because they just cannot be bothered. Their reasons for this may be many and varied. Others may not achieve because they have entered a course of study merely to please their parents. They find they are following a path that was not discussed with them, but that it was assumed they would follow. They did this dutifully through their school years to find themselves at college or university with the dreadful realisation that this is not what they wanted; this group of people may lack motivation.

You don't have to be a mastermind to be able to study and to achieve a reasonable standard. You do, though, have to approach your studies with an attitude that will enable you to help yourself. Often the only thing that will get in between you and your goal is, unfortunately, you. Adopting an appropriate attitude for some means change. Change can be an uncomfortable and sometimes painful experience. It is said that you first make your habits and then your habits make you. Not all of your habits are necessarily conducive to effective study.

Personal filters

Knight (2002) asks if, having bought a car, you suddenly become aware of the other cars around you that are of the same type. Here she is referring to the filters of conscious-ness that can affect you, often on a subconscious level. This is about how you perceive things. If you have a relative who has become ill, you may become acutely aware of that particular illness and notice newspaper articles or radio programmes on the subject. Consideration of your personal filters can provide a useful insight into your approach to study, because they enable you to see how you typically view things, situations and people and how, as a result, you may react in various situations.

An example of a personal filter is to:

Sort for good •————————————————• **Sort for bad**

The personal filter can be heard in the language people use. For example, 'the glass is half empty' is interpreted as sorting for bad, whereas 'the glass is half full' is considered as sorting for good. Generally you interpret 'the glass is half full' to mean a good thing, as the person is viewed as being optimistic, and 'the glass is half empty' as a bad thing, as the person is viewed as being pessimistic. As a generalisation, some people go through life noticing everything that is wrong. They look at things and only notice imperfections. If they observe a sunny day, they perceive that they may burn in the sun. On a cloudy day they may see nothing but impending rain.

Conversely, the person situated at the other end of the line (bipolar axis) sorts for good and notices the positive attributes of, for example, that sunny day. For them it is sunny and therefore they can get out and enjoy it. If they experience a cloudy day they are pleased that it is not raining. However, a person can be at any part of the line and some are quite at home in the middle. Consideration of personal filters is useful because it enables you to understand yourself and your approach to study.

Similarity •————————————————• Difference

Those filtering for 'similarity' would identify the common traits in, for example, objects, situations or people. The similarities would leap out at you and make you aware that, perhaps, all the objects in front of you were a shade of brown or most of the situations we found most pleasant involved eating. Perhaps, when you observe a group of people, you may notice that they were all aged between 25 and 35 years or they bought their clothes from a certain shop. Alternatively, those programmed to filter out everything except difference would be aware that, of all the objects they are observing, one was slightly taller than the rest. When they observe a group of people, they may notice those who were not wearing clothes from a particular shop. It is worth bearing in mind that the personal filter is contextual and an individual can be anywhere along the axis. Personal filters affect the way in which you relate to your own individual model of the world.

REFLECTIVE TASK

Consider the following and mark the line (the bipolar axis) where you think you are in relation to your studies:

1.

Away from •————————————————• *Towards*

Those who are inclined to move 'away from' identify what should be avoided and take action to keep away from it. They are quick to notice what is wrong with something or what is apparently out of place. They filter things in terms of what they don't want.	*Those who move 'towards' are focused on their goals; they see what they want and go for it. They tend to be good at prioritising and are motivated to achieve. They filter things in terms of what they want.*

2.

Specific •————————————————• *General*

Those who are content to work with small pieces of material. They look for detail and facts, which enable them to gradually build towards making sense of the big picture. They deal in small of chunks.	*Those who like the big picture and can view it in its entirety. They deal in the abstract or theoretical and have little time for specific detail. They deal in big chunks.*

3.

Internal frame of reference •————————• **External frame of reference**

Internally referenced people know what they like, recognise their own competence and can identify their own standards. They rely upon themselves and are proactive.

Externally referenced people rely on others for direction or instruction. They look to others for a set of standards. They rely upon others and are reactive.

4.

Possibility •————————• **Necessity**

People with this characteristic are inclined to do things just because they can. They speculate about the possibilities and about what they can achieve in life.

People with this characteristic are inclined to do things because they must. They may enrol on a course because they require the necessary qualification for a new job.

5.

In time •————————• **Through time**

To these people what is important is now, at this moment. There is little concept of time beyond now. There is no thought about saving money for tomorrow. These people often turn up late for appointments.

To these people what matters here is a sense of time in a linear form. They may consider going without for the sake of tomorrow. They are acutely aware of time to the extent that they turn up early and wait outside a meeting just to be on time.

6.

Self •————————• **Others**

Those who sort for self ensure that they benefit from their own and others' actions. Even if they appear to be doing another person a favour, you can guarantee that there is something in it for themselves.

Those who sort for others are altruistic and are concerned with the well-being of others. They ask for nothing in return and receive pleasure from the act of giving in one form or another.

7.

Right/Wrong •————————• **Accepting**

Those who view everything in terms of right or wrong. It is as if they are in possession of the book of rules, which is written in terms of things being either right or wrong. There can be nothing in between and there is a tendency to expect others to agree with their opinion.

Those who don't view things in terms of right and wrong, but simply accept things as they are. There is no value given to things, however attributes are identified and valued, but not judged. They possess unconditional positive regard for others.

8.

Match	Mismatch
Those who act as chameleons in life, matching others' language patterns, body language and dress and the values of individuals and groups. They can be all things to all people and are viewed, sometimes unfairly, as insincere.	*Those who will do whatever it takes to ensure the various attributes of the other are not matched or reflected by themselves in any way. They can be viewed as being disagreeable or argumentative, sometimes unfairly.*

9.

Independent	Cooperative
Those who prefer to work in isolation and to be left alone. They will take sole responsibility for their actions. They find other people an unnecessary distraction.	*Those who prefer the company of others and are happy to function in a team. They are motivated by shared responsibility, recognising that successful projects occur as a result of everyone's involvement.*

10.

Rule-bound	Rule-free
Those who accept rules and require them to function. They are best suited to working in large organisations where adhering to procedures is necessary. They may feel the need to advise others upon how they should act.	*Those who don't do rules. If rules do exist, they will bend them, break them or ignore them. They feel no need to follow given procedures or protocols. If others wish to break the rules too, they probably would not even notice.*

The study of personal filters is useful, because they enable you to think about yourself and your habits. Remember, though, they are context reliant; in other words, you will exhibit different behaviours in different locations and with different people. What is important is that you recognise what you are doing.

When considering your attitude towards study, consider the personal filter involving 'sorting for good . . . bad'. For many there is a tendency to sort for bad; it appears to be a natural thing to do. But if all you ever do is judge your course and everything in it negatively, your world can become negative. You may judge yourself as harshly as you do others, but again this may do little to engender a positive outlook in your study. If you have made up your mind that you want to exhibit a positive attitude to study, consider where you are in between the two ends of the bipolar axis. If you are towards the sorting for bad area, you should make a conscious effort to review your attitude.

Steps of competence

Your studies are not restricted to sitting in a darkened room, alone with your books. Study is also a social activity and therefore, to be successful, you will benefit from thinking how you relate to others and to yourself. Thinking about you, your studies, your relationships and your course is an important activity. Roffey-Barentsen and Malthouse refer to the principles of a psycholateral approach to thinking, observing that:

> *A psycholateral approach provides an informed method of thinking, enabling you to consider any given incident or situation from a variety of perspectives and contexts, before arriving at a conclusion and importantly before deciding on any course of action.*

(2009, p42)

As you enter your own world of study, you may begin to notice that different topics will demand of you various study techniques to match the variety of perspectives and contexts involved in each topic. For example, the task of honing a skill will require a different approach to that of acquiring and remembering facts. Your task is to employ an informed method of thinking appropriate to each subject. By now you will recognise that there is more than one way to study a topic; your task is to use the most appropriate method for any given situation. As you study you will develop skills that will improve as you practise them. To do this you will find that your level of competence changes as you improve as a learner.

Five steps of competence

Figure 1.1 shows the five steps of the conscious steps model. There are a number of variations, many of which use just four steps (Roffey-Barentsen and Malthouse, 2009).

- **Step 1: Unconscious incompetence.** Before you embarked on your studies it is possible that you were not aware of what exactly what was involved in the process. At this stage you could have been described as being unconsciously incompetent. In other words, not only were there aspects of study skills you were unable to accomplish, you were unaware of this fact.

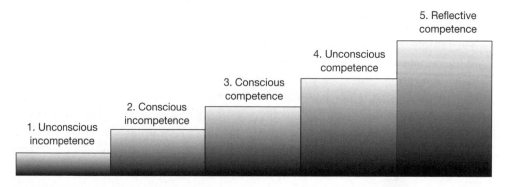

Figure 1.1 Conscious steps model

- **Step 2: Conscious incompetence.** As you begin your studies, you could become aware that certain areas of study skills require attention. This stage is referred to as conscious incompetence. Now you are aware of your level of ability.

- **Step 3: Conscious competence.** Conscious competence refers to the stage at which you have become proficient, but at which you still need to give conscious thought to the process. You have to remind yourself of some strategies before using them.

- **Step 4: Unconscious competence.** At this level, you are so competent that you do not need to give the activity of study much thought. In fact you are so good at it that you can do it without thinking about what you are doing, and you are said to be unconsciously competent.

- **Step 5: Reflective competence.** This is the position where you make a conscious effort to review your ability. For example, new ideas in relation to study skills could be written about and you could consider assimilating these into your study. Reflective competence describes the process of thinking about what you have done and asking if what you are doing is in fact the most appropriate way. You do this without needing to go back to conscious incompetence.

The levels of competence can apply to many educational activities, for example learning to drive a car, using new computer software, utilising an unfamiliar procedure, etc. What is useful about these steps is that they give you the opportunity to think about and identify your own development and level of ability. The process of thinking about your own development is referred to as reflective practice and is described below.

Reflective practice

What is reflective practice? Reflective practice involves thinking about an experience so that, the next time you meet the same or a similar experience, you can do better. This process consists of you thinking about what you have done, considering what your options are, planning for the next occasion and then doing it; it is cyclic in nature. The concept of thinking about thinking is not new. One of the theorists associated with reflective practice is Kolb, who introduced his four-stage model of learning in 1984. He used technical language when describing his model, so in Figure 1.2 the language has been altered to offer a more accessible version.

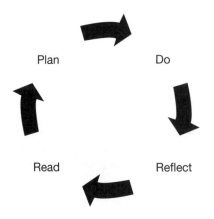

Figure 1.2
A simplified version of Kolb's learning cycle

What does this mean for you? How does it relate to your own individual study skills? As can be seen, the model comprises four stages and it can be applied to any activity. The activity chosen here is writing an assignment.

1. Do it	You complete your first assignment; it is handed in, marked and returned to you. You are disappointed with your mark and want to do better the next time.
2. Reflect on it	You read the feedback and think about the lecturer's observations. You think about what it was you were trying to do and the words you chose to express yourself. You consider which aspects went well, what went less well, what you did, what you didn't do, the reasons for that, etc. You identify some topics that require further attention.
3. Read up on it	You attend your library, search the intranet or internet or speak to your tutor or your peers. Here you identify the criteria for writing at the appropriate level. If you don't understand something, you don't leave it there, you find out.
4. Plan the next stage	Now you have acquainted yourself with the theory and suggested good practice, you are able to plan exactly how you will design your next assignment.

Reece and Walker (2007) point out that the importance of this model is that it can be started at any stage and it combines reflection with experience. This model can be very useful for people who wish to take an active part in improving their own study skills. According to Roffey-Barentsen and Malthouse (2009, p6), 'The reason for this is that it is clear, unambiguous and follows a logical progression.' For example, if you felt that you knew nothing about writing an assignment other than what you had picked up at school, it may be a good idea to start at the 'Read up on it' stage; this would equip you with the knowledge necessary to construct an assignment. Next, you would move to 'Plan the next stage'. This would be achieved by:

- identifying the criteria;
- ascertaining your argument;
- detailing the various sections;
- identifying relevant literature;
- writing out an overall plan of the assignment.

Next would be to 'Do it' by writing the assignment and then to 'Reflect on it' by reading the feedback and thinking about what you have done, why you have done it, etc. But it does not finish there; reflective practice is an ongoing process in which you always try to do a little better on the next occasion. Essentially it means that you, as learner, take responsibility for your own learning. The main advantage of this system is that you take responsibility for yourself. You think about what you have done and how you have done it, you then read up about it to find more information and decide how you will do it differently on the next occasion. It has been suggested that the only person we really listen to is ourselves; here it is put into practice. This approach to learning is called the student-centred approach, because the learner is at the heart of the process and assumes responsibility for their own learning. Obviously you are not alone while engaging in reflective practice. Your tutor will be there to advise you, or you may have a mentor. However, ultimately you decide how well you have done and what is required of you on the next occasion in order to make your learning as effective as it can be.

Below are two examples of reflective practice entries. You can see that they are not complicated and are designed to enable you to make sense of the situation you may find yourself within.

Reflective practice entry 1

1. **Do it** (What exactly?)	2. **Reflect on it**
Today we were introduced to citing and referencing and how, if we want to use a passage from a book, we can do it without plagiarism.	At first I thought I understood. It's always like that in class; at the time it makes perfect sense and then later I forget and it is not so clear. I am not sure when to put the page number in and when not to. There are two rules for this but I can't remember which is which.
4. **Plan the next stage**	3. **Read up on it**
I will use just direct quotes in the next assignment, just so I get used to using them. Then, later, I will use the other method with just the author's ideas.	I have read up in the study skills book about how to do it. It says that, if you are quoting directly, word for word, you must use the year and the page number. If you are just using the idea, you just use the date. That is not as difficult as I remembered.

Overleaf is a blank chart for you to use for your first reflective entry; photocopy this to use yourself. Using reflective practice regularly helps make sense of the situations you can find yourself in. The topics you choose to record can be anything from your academic studies to social incidents or financial considerations. Writing things down can also be cathartic.

Reflective practice entry 2

1. **Do it** (What exactly?)	2. **Reflect on it**
We were told that the best marks would be allocated to those who used analysis in their writing. No one mentioned what it was and I can't remember, but I didn't want to look an idiot in front of the others: I bet half of them couldn't remember either.	I should have asked, but they were all nodding their heads and looking very knowledgeable. I must have been there when they described it, but I can't for the life of me remember what it is all about. I still think I did the right thing though; I just don't want to look a loser.
4. **Plan the next stage**	3. **Read up on it**
I will draw up an assignment plan and ensure that each stage of analysis is discrete. This will draw attention to the fact that I know what I am talking about.	I have read up in the study skills book how to do it. It says that analysis is all about breaking the subject down into the component parts and then identifying how they relate to each other. This is not rocket science; I can do that.

1. **Do it** (What exactly?)	2. **Reflect on it**
4. **Plan the next stage**	3. **Read up on it**

C H A P T E R   S U M M A R Y

This chapter has considered the difficulty some people experience when getting started. To this end a questionnaire was offered to help you identify aspects of study skills that were pertinent to you. Next, motivation was considered, highlighting the differences between extrinsic and intrinsic positions, and seven good habits of motivation were offered. Time management was examined and an activity matrix was used to identify the time available to you for study. Activity scheduling described the importance of planning activities and an example was offered. Concentration was considered in relation to finding a suitable environment for study and techniques to keep your mind on the task in hand. The importance of chunking work into manageable sections was highlighted, as was the importance of taking regular breaks. Cultivating a positive attitude to study was considered and the concept of personal filters was introduced. The five steps of competence were discussed for you to identify your own progress. Lastly, the benefit of reflective practice was highlighted as a tool to assist your learning by questioning your assumptions and researching solutions.

REFERENCES

Cottrell, S (1999) *The Study Skills Handbook*. Hampshire: Palgrave.

Knight, S (2002) *NLP at Work: The Difference that Makes the Difference in Business*, 2nd edition. London: Nicholas Brealey.

Ormrod, JE (2008) *Human Learning*, 5th edition. Upper Saddle River, NJ: Pearson.

Reece, I and Walker, S (2007) *Teaching, Training and Learning: A Practical Guide*, 6th edition. Sunderland: Business Education Publishers.

Roffey-Barentsen, J and Malthouse, R (2009) *Reflective Practice in the Lifelong Learning Sector*. Exeter: Learning Matters.

Tracy, B (2004) *Eat That Frog*. London: Hodder Headline.

USEFUL WEBSITE

www.skillsfor justice-nosfinder.com (Skills for Justice, National Occupational Standards for Policing and Law Enforcement 2008)

2 Reading and making notes

CHAPTER OBJECTIVES

By the end of this chapter you will be able to:

- become a more selective reader;
- explain the reading process and appropriate reading speeds;
- select strategies to improve your comprehension of a text;
- identify suitable strategies for making notes;
- distinguish between making notes from lectures, books and the internet;
- employ the Cornell method of note-taking.

LINKS TO STANDARDS

This chapter provides opportunities for links with the following Skills for Justice, National Occupational Standards (NOS) for Policing and Law Enforcement 2008.

AB1.1   Communicate effectively with people.
AE1.1   Maintain and develop your own knowledge and competence.

Introduction

Paying attention to detail, and the ability to read and record facts accurately and to assimilate those facts, will serve you well both as a student and as a police officer. From the start of your study you will engage in reading and writing in certain styles, progressing to writing academically. Later, the principles of this academic writing will inform your professional practice in the Police Service, where you will be expected to read:

- reports;

- legislation;

- procedure;

- instructions;

- briefing sheets;

- crime reports;

- intelligence reports;

- gazettes;

- notices;

- national occupational standards;

- books;

- crime scene logs;

- guidelines.

Each of these documents will be written in a different style because they will have been written for different purposes. No matter what form the writing takes, the common task is to glean as much relevant information from the writing as possible. What is relevant will depend on what you are reading and what you want from the text; for example, do you require the definition of a concept or law or are you searching the text for someone's name? Similarly, the quality and style of your writing will differ in accordance with the type of document you are preparing. This chapter will provide you with various reading strategies and will assist you with writing in the form of note-taking.

Reading at an academic level

You probably read every day. This can be the headlines in a newspaper, signs on the motorway, a set of instructions, your emails, a magazine or a favourite novel. However, reading while studying for a degree is different. You may have to read more than you are used to, as most academic courses require a substantial amount of reading. Further, the content may be different. Some of the textbooks or journals are dry or difficult to understand, using complex concepts. Finally, you have to remember it all: a daunting task. The next part of this chapter gives you some guidelines on how to manage these key issues.

What to read, how much and where to find it

You may feel overwhelmed by the amount of reading that you are expected to do for your degree. Some students perceive the reading as a huge obstacle – a mountain that is in their way. If this is how you feel, you may need to consider your attitude to reading. After all, the purpose of reading is to become informed, which will help you when writing an assignment or essay, or preparing for an examination or presentation. You need to find out who the experts are on the subject and what they say. Therefore, you will probably start with some background reading, to explore the subject, core themes and issues. Most lecturers will give you a reading list for each module you study, and are likely to indicate what is 'essential' reading and what are more general titles. If you are provided with an alphabetical, general list, don't be put off but ask your tutor to identify key texts.

Time management

To make best use of your time, you need to be selective in your reading. You may be used to reading a book from cover to cover, starting at the beginning and finishing at 'the end'. However, when reading academic textbooks you hardly ever have to do this. First of all, you need to decide what exactly you want to find out about – decide on a keyword. Don't just go by the title of a book, but also have a look in the index, identify in which chapter or on what pages your keyword features, and start reading that chapter or those pages. It could be that, although the book is mentioned on your reading list, you only need to read that one chapter. If you have to read the whole book or if the book is more general and it's not clear which chapters to focus on, start by reading the information on the back cover, known as the 'blurb', and the introduction. Next, look at each chapter. Most of the time the first and last paragraph of a chapter are the most useful, as they summarise what the chapter will cover or has covered. After this, you'll find it much easier to identify which chapters to focus on more closely.

Once you have started reading, you may want to follow up some ideas or concepts, taking you away from the reading list. An author may cite (make reference to) another publication. Full details of that publication can usually be found in the reference list or bibliography at the end of a chapter, or at the end of the book. This makes it easier for you to further research your topic. Overall, it's best to start with the most recent publication you can find. Journals are published at regular intervals during the year and are therefore more likely to contain the latest information and developments on your subject. Articles in journals usually start with an 'abstract', which is a summary of the article. Reading these abstracts gives you enough information to decide whether you need to read the whole article or not.

PRACTICAL TASK

Choose an academic book. We suggest Police Law *by English and Card (2009). Find the blurb and introduction. Next, look at the index and try to see how closely the index reflects the blurb.*

Where do you find the information?

Books

Certain important key texts you will use over and over again, as they form the basis for your course, and you should purchase these yourself. Often there is a bookshop on site that stocks or can order textbooks for you. However, it is unlikely that you will buy all the books on your reading list. Therefore, as soon as you are enrolled on to your course, you need to register with the learning resource centre (LRC) or library. Textbooks or reference books are arranged by subject. The subject is given a number, with most institutions making use of the Dewey decimal classification system. For instance, all books on Social Science are given the number 300, which is then further classified (e.g. Law is 340). The numbers are displayed on the spine of the book and there are usually signs in the LRC directing you to the right shelves for your subject area. The LRC will also have a catalogue, where you can search for publications by name or, if you don't know the full title, by keyword in the title, or by author. Your search will give you the title of the book, its author(s) and the Dewey classification number, so you can easily locate it in the LRC.

Journals

Journals are usually kept in a separate area. Current copies may be on display, whereas past copies may be collected in numbered volumes. Bear in mind that not all LRCs allow students to take journals out on loan. Some are for reference only, which means you can access them only in the LRC. If an LRC or library induction is not included in your programme, it is worthwhile asking a member of the LRC staff to show you around and explain their systems and ways of doing things. It will save you a lot of time and possible frustration. Journals can also be accessed via the internet (see below). You can do this direct by using the computers in the LRC. To do this from home you need to get an 'Athens' password from the LRC.

Books or journals that are not stocked can be ordered for you via an inter-library loan system. In general, publications will only take a few days to arrive, but there may be a small charge for using this system. Inter-library loans are particularly useful if you would like to read the original publication of a theory that is still in use, going back to the source.

Using the internet as a resource

As well as using 'hard copies' of publications, you can also consider looking at electronic copies by accessing the internet. Further, your university or college may have its own intranet or virtual learning environment (VLE), where useful documents and resources are posted. As explained by Bedford and Wilson (2006, p32), some websites are designed specifically to help you learn new things by providing information for your course-work, essays and assignments, whereas others, such as the Home Office site (http://police.homeoffice.gov.uk/) keep you up to date with new developments in your subject. Although the internet offers a wealth of information, most of it free, you must consider the reliability of the information. Books and academic journals are reviewed by experts in the field before publication. Therefore, they make a reliable source. Entries on the internet can be published by anyone and changed at any time. Therefore, be careful not to use them as the sole source for your essays or assignments.

So, to manage your reading you have to be selective.

- Read what is relevant to your topic.
- Start reading the most recent publications.
- Make sure your source is reliable.

The reading process

Now that you have selected what you need to read, it is useful to look at the reading process. The best way is to start reading and then take time to reflect on it.

- How did you feel about the reading?
- How much time did it take to read the article/chapter?
- Did you understand it all or were there words/concepts you weren't familiar with?
- How much have you remembered?

Reading is not a one-way process. It is an interaction between you and the text. Therefore, your reading is influenced by your own characteristics as well as by the characteristics of the text, such as the size and style of the font. A whole page crammed with dense writing can be off-putting, regardless of its content. The author's writing style and the difficulty of the concepts or ideas presented also play a part. Some styles are more accessible, while others are more difficult to follow or just do not appeal to you.

For how you deal with this, it's over to you. A positive frame of mind will undoubtedly help. Chambers and Northedge (2008, p73) point out that you will learn best if you take an interest in what the text is about. Your previous or background knowledge also have an influence. A topic where you are familiar with the language or jargon used is easier to read about than a new one. Also, if you have read a lot by the same author, you become familiar with the structure of this author's writing, so you will know where to find key elements of the text. The above suggests that the more you read, the easier it becomes.

Reading speed

Finally, there is your own reading ability, for instance the speed at which you read. Could it be improved and how can you achieve that? Cottrell (2008, p120) designed the following method to check reading speed.

- Find something familiar to read.
- Set a timer for ten minutes.
- Read for ten minutes at a speed that allows you to understand what you read.
- Count how many words you read.
- Divide this number by ten, to find out how many words you read in one minute.
- Use this strategy for a number of different texts.

PRACTICAL TASK

Try the Cottrell reading test. How did you do?

Cottrell suggests that, if you read fewer than 200–250 words per minute, even with texts that are clear and interesting, you may want to increase your reading speed. Note that this figure is only a guideline – other authors suggest different, lower word counts, down to 40 words per minute for reading a difficult text (Chambers and Northedge, 2008, p84). To be able to speed up your reading, you need to identify what is slowing you down.

REFLECTIVE TASK

Consider how the following areas affect your reading speed.

- *Time: At what time do you read; is this at the end of the day when you feel tired or stressed; or do you set a time that you keep free for reading, ideally when you are not tired?*

- *Environment: What is the environment like; do you read on a crowded train, making use of every available minute, or during your lunchtime in a noisy canteen, or in your living room, surrounded by members of your family (including children) who are chatting, watching television or a DVD, or listening to their favourite music, or in the quiet area of the LRC? Although some people like some background noise, keep distractions to a minimum.*

- *Reading aloud: If you are an auditory learner, which means you learn best from hearing and listening, you may prefer to read a passage out loud; however, reading silently is quicker, so train yourself to do this.*

- *Tracing words with your finger: Some students like to trace each word as they read, so as not to lose their place; others use a ruler for the same purpose. A more efficient strategy is to move your finger directly down the page in a straight line.*

- *Words you do not know: Should you look up difficult words in a dictionary? Doing this may help you to make sense of a sentence or paragraph, but it will also slow you down and it interrupts the flow. Can you make a guess at what a word might mean? Sometimes it is enough to look at a word and consider any prefixes or suffixes.*

- *Jumping letters: If you find that letters or words jump around, making reading difficult, it's probably best to speak to your tutor. It may be that you are on the dyslexic spectrum, which affects people in different ways. Sometimes a coloured overlay, most commonly yellow or blue, may help. However, do seek advice.*

Three stages of reading

We read at different speeds when reading for different purposes. Turner et al. (2008, p46) recognise three stages of reading, especially if the reading is for an essay or assignment.

1. The early stage of reading is the most thorough and slow, as your aim is to learn about the topic.

2. In the middle stage, as you know more about the topic, you can be more precise in your selection of sources; therefore, your reading is faster.

3. In the final stage, you only need to check specific points or follow up certain ideas, which is usually a fast process.

Four types of reading

An alternative theory puts forward four types of reading with associated speeds.

1. **Systematic** reading is used if you have to evaluate, summarise or paraphrase the material. It is a careful, relatively slow process.

2. **Standard** reading is used if you have to answer specific questions or if you need to be able to tell someone else about the material you have just read.

3. **Scanning** is a faster process used to get the general idea of the material. It can be useful to scan the first sentence of each paragraph for keywords, as it will give you the gist of the topics or issues dealt with.

4. **Skimming** is faster still and is a technique that can be used when you're searching for something in particular.

So how fast you read depends on:

- how much you already know about the subject;

- your attitude;

- the environment;

- the difficulty of the text and how it is presented;

- the purpose of your reading.

Finally, there is no ideal reading speed. As explained by Chambers and Northedge (2008, p86), the skill lies in being able to 'pitch your reading speed according to the purpose and the degree of challenge presented by the text'.

Strategies to improve comprehension

The purpose of reading is not usually to be able to remember a whole text, word by word, but to understand and make sense of what you read. You know you are reading effectively when you are able to form thoughts and ideas based on the material you have read. To continue reading without understanding or comprehension is wasting your time; you need to address the gaps as they occur, either by rereading, slowing down your reading speed or by looking up words you do not know. Even so, it has probably happened to us all: you reach the end of a paragraph or page but you don't know what you have been reading – the content hasn't registered.

There are some strategies that you can employ to avoid this. The main point is that you have to be an active reader and engage with the text. To increase your comprehension you need to look at the bigger picture, identifying the text's key ideas and findings. Try predicting, making educated guesses about thoughts, outcomes or conclusions. As you read, your predictions are confirmed or denied. If they turn out to be invalid, you make new predictions. This constant process helps you become involved with the author's thinking and helps you learn.

You need to make inferences and to draw comparisons and conclusions. When you relate your existing knowledge to the new information, you're making it part of your framework of ideas. Such related experiences help you digest new material. Further, you need to recognise patterns and relationships between statements or arguments. In order to do this, you need to read critically, asking questions as you read. Sometimes you may have to reread a passage before you can summarise the main points.

PRACTICAL TASK

Carefully read a passage from one of your key texts. We suggest Blackstone's Police Manual 2010: Volume 4, General Police Duties, *4.8 Weapons, 4.8.2 'Having offensive weapon in public place' (Hutton and McKinnon, 2009, p300). Imagine you have to explain the text to someone else. What are you going to say? Practise this out loud. Were you able to remember the material and express it in your own words?*

A useful technique is to change the headings into questions that you then need to answer. Rephrase each paragraph in your own words. For example, what does the law prohibit in relation to offensive weapons in a public place? What is meant by the term 'has with him'? What is a public place within the meaning of this Act? What does the term 'offensive weapon' mean? While you are reading, consider writing notes in the margin or highlighting key ideas. Using a motor skill will help you remember.

PRACTICAL TASK

The heading for this part of the chapter is 'Strategies to improve comprehension'. Turning this into a question gives you: 'What are the strategies to improve comprehension?' Now, answer this question, using your own words.

Critical reading

As you read you have to distinguish between what is a fact and what is the opinion of the author – you have to read critically. This is not always easy, as some authors can have very strong opinions that may come across as facts. The key difference between facts and opinions is that facts can be verified or checked for accuracy. Opinions, on the other hand, cannot. They are what someone thinks. Although opinions cannot be verified, academic authors should back their opinions with evidence, facts and reason, to convince the reader that they are valid opinions. Sometimes you may not agree with what you're reading or with what the author is trying to convince you of. If that's the case, Chambers and Northedge (2008, p81) advise you to distance yourself from those hostile or uncomfortable feelings. They argue that, if you want to access a body of knowledge, you have to be prepared to get alongside the writers and follow their thoughts. When you disagree with a text, write down your criticisms and counter-arguments point by point. This will help you if you want to use the material in a critical analysis or evaluation.

So, you can improve your comprehension of reading new material by being an active and critical reader, engaging with the text.

- **Before you start reading**, scan the text first to become familiar with the material and to activate any prior knowledge.

- **While reading**, predict, ask questions, make inferences and draw comparisons. Write down information and make notes, including a counter-argument if necessary.

- **After reading**, explain what you have read to someone else. Verbalising the material in your own words will help activate your long-term memory. Reflect on and review what you have read. Link new ideas with what you already know.

Making notes

There are specific times when it is good practice to make notes: when you attend a lecture, lesson or seminar, or when researching from books, journals and papers. As a police officer you will be expected to make notes as soon after an incident as you can, while it is still fresh in your mind. Later these notes may form the basis of a statement used in court. The principles of note-taking in a lecture are similar to those that apply when writing up your recollections of an incident.

Lectures, lessons and seminars

When you attend a lecture, lesson or seminar it is important to take notes. You may be tempted not to bother; however, when you get home you may not remember exactly what was discussed. When taking notes you are investing in the future, looking towards a time when you need to call on not just the bare facts but the subtle influences, contexts and comparisons.

Note-taking in different circumstances
The method of note-taking can alter depending on the circumstances. For example, in a lecture, which as defined by Reece and Walker (2007, p26) is a 'one-way communication by the teacher with no feedback from students', little interaction is expected between the lecturer and the students. Therefore, you have plenty of time to take notes. On the other hand, if the session is more interactive, you may have less time for note-taking. A seminar, where you research a topic and present the findings to other students (Reece and Walker, 2007, p123), will allow even less time to write notes. The style of your notes will be influenced by the time you have available.

Prior to a lecture
- Identify the existence of any handouts, PowerPoint presentations or other prepared material.

- Make sure you have paper and pens with you.

- Take a look at the criteria for the assignment, as this will identify some of your own questions that you may want answered.

How much information should you record? Attempting to write every word spoken verbatim will lead only to frustration. Therefore, you have to be selective in the notes you take. As a minimum it is advised that 'your note-taking strategy for lectures should include getting down on paper the broad structure of the lecture' (Walmsley, 2006, p54).

PRACTICAL TASK

Watch the News programme on the television. Practise taking notes on what is said. Over time you will be able to distil the salient points.

During the lecture
Try not to miss the beginning of a lecture as you may miss vital clues to guide your thoughts through and around the subject. Lecturers often introduce the major points or ideas at the start of the session or display the learning outcomes. These act as signposts, enabling you to grasp the direction of that session. This will indicate what is worth recording and helps you select topics for headings and subheadings, forming the framework for your notes.

Stay organised; for instance, when you are provided with handouts make sure you identify them. For example, at the top right of the page you could write: HO2/22.11.10, indicating that this is the second handout of the lecture delivered on the 22 November 2010. Remember to cross-reference the handouts within your notes, to recognise exactly where they fit. Alternatively, you can make notes on your handouts; some lecturers provide PowerPoints with blank notes pages for you to use. However, guard against your notes being so disparate that you cannot make sense of them.

Presentation of your notes
You are making notes to jog your memory, so it is essential that your notes are well laid out, represent the subject delivered and are readable. The layout of your notes often depends on personal preference. Here are some options.

Write and flight method
Quite simply you write what you feel is important and then fly off to the next topic or point of interest. Notes will be brief and may lack structure. However, this method enables you listen to what is being said, concentrating on the lecture rather than making detailed notes and, thereby, potentially missing salient points.

Cornell method
A more structured approach is the Cornell method, introduced by Walter Pauk (1997) from Cornell University. For this you fold or mark the paper lengthwise so that it has two

columns, with the column on the left about half the size of the one on the right. Then follow five steps.

1. **Record** – In the right-hand column: notes are taken at the time and are as full as possible, ensuring that all the key points and ideas are recorded.

2. **Reduce** – In the left-hand column: notes are condensed into a form suitable for you. By using your own words you concentrate the information into a form that will suit your ability to learn. Direct quotes or dates should remain just as they are.

3. **Recite** – Cover the original notes in the first part and recall the facts, quotes, questions, etc.; these can be said out loud. The intention is not to learn the words verbatim, but to get to the meaning of the words in a way that makes sense to you. Then, uncover the notes and compare what you thought you had said to what is written. This can be repeated as often as is necessary to learn.

4. **Reflect** – In the right-hand column: ponder why things are as they are, asking a series of whys. This may assist your enquiring mind, when every time you get to an answer, you ask yourself why that is; try to examine the situation to the root cause. Engaging in reflective practice enables you to view a situation differently. Hatton and Smith (1995) in Roffey-Barentsen and Malthouse (2009, p85) refer to this process as 'a stepping back from the events'. By doing this you are better able to view the whole picture and from this gain an insight into the topic you are considering. At a deeper level you may engage in 'critical reflection' (2009, p85), where events are explained from multiple perspectives. It is only by taking time to think about the material that you will be able to engage in any form of reflective practice.

5. **Review** – Return to what you have written each week, just to ensure you can keep the information fresh in your mind.

On paper it looks like this:

2. Reduce Reduce the original record to concise facts, quotes or questions; these should be in your own words.	**1. Record** Record any facts, phrases, quotes and ideas as fully as is practical.
3. Recite Covering the original record, recite each fact, quote or question repeatedly.	**4 and 5. Reflect and Review** Reflect on the meaning and correlations of the subject, asking a series of whys. Return to these notes frequently over time in order to keep them fresh in your mind.

PRACTICAL TASK

Practise the Cornell method at your next lecture and see how it suits you. Remember, the more you practise the better you will get.

Speed of thought and speed of speech

When your lecturer is speaking, you may be able to jump ahead in your thoughts. By doing this you will be predicting what the person is about to say. The danger is that, while you are engaging in this anticipation, you are not actually listening as fully as you might. As a result it is possible that you could miss something that will assist your understanding. If you do find yourself anticipating what is going to be said, check yourself and bring yourself back to the here and now.

Abbreviating

The acronym KISS stands for Keep It Short and Simple. This applies well to your note-taking. You may be short of time in a lecture as the words come hurtling towards you and it may feel that it is difficult to keep up. A common coping strategy is to use abbreviations or a form of code. Remember, abbreviating should only ever be used when you are actually taking notes for your own use and never for academic writing or within any police document.

Whatever you do, it is a good idea to be consistent, otherwise you may forget what was written or you may confuse yourself. Some useful abbreviations are shown in Table 2.1.

Table 2.1 Some useful abbreviations

bc	because	**@**	around/circa
ch	chapter	**edn**	edition
etc.	et cetera/and other things/and so on	**i.e.**	That is/that is to say
e.g.	for example	**NB**	nota bene/note well
p.	page	**para.**	paragraph
&	and	**=**	equals/as a result of/which meant that/which means
>	greater than/more than	**<**	less than
vs	versus/in opposition to/against	**C20**	twentieth century
≠	is not equal to	**no.**	number

Another useful style of abbreviation is text speak, the shorthand used by people when they send a text message (see Table 2.2).

Table 2.2 Some examples of text speak

b	be	**txt**	text	**4**	for
r	are	**L8r**	later	**b4**	before
y	why	**ne**	any	**M8**	mate
8	ate	**c**	see	**U2**	**you too**
2	to or too	**u**	you	**cuz**	because
der4	therefore	**n**	and	**m**	am

Source: O2 (2009).

PRACTICAL TASK

Work out the following:

l12cu

Cu l8r k?

w8 4me @da rvp

(Source: HardwareGeeks.com, 2009)

(The answers are given at the end of the chapter.)

Obviously because this form of communication is derived from text conversations not all the words shown above are going to be useful in a lecture. However many can be adapted to suit you as you make your notes or alternatively you can invent your own.

Twenty rules for writing notes

Do:

1. arrive with the intention of learning;

2. keep an open mind;

3. engage your brain;

4. be alert;

5. ask for clarity if you do not understand;

6. be positive;

7. write only what you require;

8. develop a form of abbreviation;

9. pay attention;;

10. think and link to what you already know.

Do not:

11. write absolutely everything down;

12. prejudge the lecturer;

13. speak without first thinking;

14. become distracted

15. record the lesson without permission;

16. let your opinions get in your way

17. think that you know everything there is to know about a subject;

18. get in the way of your own or others' learning;

19. text;

20. argue with the lecturer.

Mapping

Mapping is a method used to set out ideas pictorially to gain a better understanding of a situation or idea. Tree maps, concept maps and mind maps rely on the use of words, although icons or pictures are not precluded.

Tree maps

Starting with the trunk, which represents the main overarching topic, your notes follow the larger branches and then the smaller branches as the topic is explained (see Figure 2.1). This is a useful way of identifying how things combine to form a whole and, conversely, how things branch out. The larger branches are representative of strands of ideas or topics, while the smaller branches identify extra information that is directly related to the larger branches.

Concept maps

In a concept map ideas are placed on paper and lines are drawn between the ideas to indicate where relationships exist (see Figure 2.2). The advantage of a concept map is that it presents you with the overall picture; it ensures you have gathered all the information available and that you don't forget anything. The disadvantage of this form of note-making is that, in order to build up the concept map, it is necessary to have an idea of the general size and nature of the topic before you embark so as to ensure there is enough space between the topics.

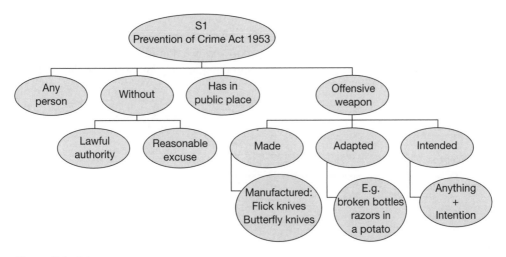

Figure 2.1 A tree map

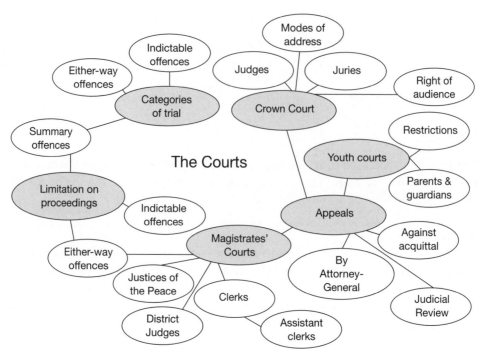

Figure 2.2 A concept map

Mind maps

Tony Buzan (2007) is credited with creating the mind map, which is similar to a concept map. However, rather than lines being drawn between ideas, here the connecting lines are directed towards a single central core (see Figure 2.3). This shows the features that have contributed to the whole. As with all mapping, it is a form of pictorial analysis. The advantage of mapping, in its various forms, is that it enables you to view a concept as a whole.

The disadvantage of making notes in a mapping form is that, if you are not made aware of the constituent parts, you do not know how much space to leave for the other strands or topics. As a result, it may mean that any mapping is made following a lecture. On the one hand, this is a positive thing as, by revisiting the material, you may learn the contents.

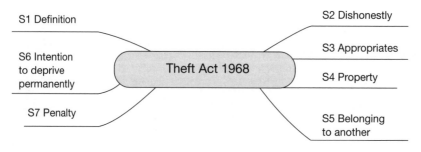

Figure 2.3 A mind map

On the other hand, you are making a note twice, which is arguably not the best use of one of your most precious resources – time.

After a lecture

After the lecture you should review your notes as soon as possible so that you do not forget what you meant if your notes are scant or difficult to read, or so that you can expand upon important points. At this stage ensure that your notes are complete, readable and sensible, for example not so long that you will never find the time to read them and not so short that they offer little assistance to you at a later date. It may be that you need to add to your notes or to make appropriate links to books or articles you have read. If you have any outstanding questions that are unanswered, make a list of these in a coloured ink and seek to resolve them. If you don't make the effort at this stage, you never will.

Often, after a period of reflective practice, you may feel that your notes require changing or amending. This is a good thing, but retain your original notes just in case you need to refer back to them for some reason. It is good practice to highlight important words and key ideas. However, use this highlighter sparingly, otherwise your page can end up being mostly yellow or bright pink, which will serve no useful purpose. Follow the advice from Pauk and revisit your notes. Arguably it is easier to retain knowledge than it is to relearn it. Obviously, as the semester progresses, this task will take longer as the amount of notes you have written increases.

Taking notes from texts

Unlike attending lectures, taking notes from books, articles and papers should be less frantic as you can work at your own pace and not that dictated by the lecturer. Books and so on are used to gather information as you research in preparation for an assignment, essay or examination. Some students write in pencil directly into the book. Do this only if the book belongs to you. There are occasions when pen is used to make notes within a library book, but this is contrary to the Criminal Damage Act 1971 and should be avoided, especially if you wish to become a police officer. If you are using library books, it is useful to fix sticky labels to indicate where helpful information may be found. These should be stuck in such a way that they project from the book so that, if you have placed handy notes on them for your own reference, they can be read. You can then quickly find the pages you require.

Citing

Citing means to use the actual words from another source, such as a book or article. Make sure you make a note of the authors' names, the title of the book, the page number, the publisher's name and the place of publishing. If you do not, when you come to referencing the material, you may have a lot of searching to do to find the exact spot in the book from which you referenced the material.

Papers and articles can take the form of entries in journals or magazines. These can be photocopied, subject to certain rules. Think about your time management; if you have time to photocopy the articles or journals, do you have the time to read them and record the information there and then? This would save you time, effort and the cost of photocopying. You can either take notes on paper or place them directly into a computer. If you do photocopy a piece of writing, again remember to make a note of which journal or paper the work is from, as this will need to be recorded within your reference section – that is, the list of all the books, articles, journals, etc. you use to write an assignment. It is useful just to write these details on the first page of your photocopy, as that way they are unlikely to be lost.

As with a lecture, the actual method of note-taking employed often comes down to personal preference. If you are unaware of the nature and size of the topic being studied, it is worthwhile considering the mapping style. Bedford and Wilson (2006, p42) suggest one benefit of this method: '[Maps] can allow you to summarise many pages of reading and you concentrate on identifying the themes.'

PRACTICAL TASK

Using a mapping system of your choice, complete a map for this chapter.

Taking notes from the internet

Taking notes from the internet is easy because in most cases you can cut and paste into your own document if you are using Word. Some documents may require more work, such as PDF files, which preserve the look and feel of the original document complete with fonts, colours, images and layout. It is a format commonly used for government publications, leaflets and forms. In order to cut the words you may have to click on the text button at the top of the page. You can then highlight the words you wish to copy and take them to your own document. This is perfectly legal and allowed as long as you acknowledge your source and add it to your reference list along with the date you accessed it. If you copy and paste part of a document and then call it your own, this is called plagiarism and is a form of theft. If you were to do this you could be expelled from your course. It is also very easy for the reader to detect, since a borrowed passage will often use a different style of language from your own and will stand out. For more information on citing and referencing see pages 50–2.

PRACTICAL TASK

Read the passage below and make brief notes, listing the salient points. Compare these to the suggested notes at the end of the exercise.

2. The purpose of a written exercise

The purpose of the written exercise is to test your ability to communicate in writing. As a police officer you will be expected to record information accurately in a form that can be understood by others. Although information and

---

communication technology (ICT) is gradually being introduced into the Police Service, there are occasions when your original notes are still written within a notebook, for example where an arrest has been made or an incident of note has taken place. Original notes are the record a police officer makes as soon as possible after an incident, during which time the details are still clear in his or her mind. These form the basis of a subsequent statement if a case is proceeded with to the appropriate court. This is often written many weeks or months after the original incident. Therefore, if the original notes are written poorly or certain words are illegible, mistakes could be made. A mistake made within the case papers can have the potential of losing a case. This is because it could throw an element of doubt on your honesty. A jury is reminded by the judge at the summing up stage of a case of what is referred to as the burden of proof. In effect, this means that, if they have any doubt as to the person's guilt, they should find the accused not guilty.

When police officers take statements from witnesses, it is the practice that the officers record their accounts in paper form; therefore, accuracy is paramount. Further, some reports, such as a road traffic collision report, are copied and forwarded to other interested parties; again it is essential that, as well as being accurate, the report is clear, coherent and comprehensive.

Other than making notes after an arrest, incident or collision, police officers are responsible for writing reports, replying to letters and recommending particular courses of action. For many of these, ICT is available, but a computer has its limitations. There are words that, although spelt correctly, may be used incorrectly – 'hours' becomes 'ours' or 'tours', etc. – and because these words are spelt correctly the computer will not necessarily identify them. It is only with careful examination of the finished product that you will be able to identify these mistakes. Recognising the difference between there, their and they're can assist your writing without the need to rely totally on the computer.

(Malthouse and Roffey-Barentsen, 2009)

Suggested brief notes:

Purpose of written excise = test written communication

PC to record info accurately → understood by others

Notebook → Original notes = soon as poss after incident still clear in mind → Become statement?

Mistakes → lose case → doubt on honesty

Witness statements taken on paper given to interested parties – must be accurate, clear, coherent, etc.

Also PCs do reports, letters, recommendations re action

ICT good but has limitations

Must look at finished report to see mistakes – can't rely on computer alone

C H A P T E R   S U M M A R Y

In this chapter we began by looking at how you can become a selective reader. The reading process and appropriate reading speeds were also examined and we provided strategies to improve your comprehension of a text. We then went on to describe some strategies for making notes, including various types of mapping. The differences between making notes in lectures and from books and the internet were also noted and we described the Cornell method of note-taking.

Answers to tasks

Texting (page 34)

I12cu	I want to see you
Cu l8r k?	See you later, ok?
w8 4me @da rvp	Wait for me at the rendezvous point

Bedford, D and Wilson, E (2006) *Study Skills for Foundation Degrees*. London: David Fulton Publishers.

Buzan, T (2007). *The Buzan Study Skills Handbook*. Harlow: BBC Active, Pearson Education.

Chambers, E and Northedge, A (2008) *The Arts Good Study Guide*. Milton Keynes: The Open University.

Cottrell, S. (2008) *The Study Skills Handbook*, 3rd edition. Basingstoke: Palgrave Macmillan.

English, J and Card, R (2009) *Police Law*, 11th edition. Oxford: Oxford University Press.

HardwareGeeks.com (2009) *Text Speak*. Available online at www.hardwaregeeks.com/board/showthread.php?t=5664 (accessed 29 March 2009).

Hutton, G and McKinnon, G (2009) *Blackstone's Police Manual: Volume 4, General Police Duties*, 12th edition. Oxford: Oxford University Press.

Malthouse, R and Roffey-Barentsen, J (2009) *Written Exercises for the Police Recruit Assessment Process*. Exeter: Learning Matters.

O2 (2009) *Business Tool Kit: A Beginners Guide to Text Speak*. Available online at http://specials.uk.msn.com/o2businesstoolkit/beginnersguidetextspeak.aspx (accessed 29 March 2009).

Pauk, W (1997) *How to Study in College*, 6th edition. Boston, MA: Houghton Mifflin.

Reece, I and Walker, S (2007) *Teaching, Training and Learning*, 6th edition. Houghton-le-Spring: Business Education Publishers.

Roffey-Barentsen, J and Malthouse, R (2009) *Reflective Practice in the Lifelong Learning Sector*. Exeter: Learning Matters.

Turner, K, Ireland, L, Krenus, B and Pointon, L (2008) *Essential Academic Skills*. South Melbourne: Oxford University Press.

Walmsley, B (2006) *Teach Yourself Good Study Skills.* London: Hodder Education.

USEFUL WEBSITES

http://articles.techrepublic.com.com/5100-10878_11-6086789.html (TechRepublic's Anatomy of Word)

http://en.wikipedia.org/wiki/Pdf_file (Wikipedia's explanation of PDFs)

http://police.homeoffice.gov.uk (new developments in the Police Service)

www.direct.gov.uk/en/Hl1/Help/DG_10014666 (Directgov's Help with PDF files)

www.dummies.com/how-to/content/notetaking-on-the-computer.html (Dummies.com's information on computer note-taking)

www.ThinkBuzan.com/uk/products/imindmap (demonstration of mind mapping software)

3 Writing skills

Introduction

While studying for your policing degree, you will be asked to produce a substantial amount of written work. This can be in the form of reports, essays or assignments. Although presentations and other activities may form part of the assessment procedure, the emphasis, in terms of assessment, is on your written work. The reason for this is that writing forms a major part of your learning process. When writing, you have to explain and justify your ideas and those of other people. This involves reading around the subject you have been asked to write about, as described in Chapter 2. Standing back and articulating your thoughts on paper will strengthen your ability to express yourself, leading to a deeper level of learning. In your writing you demonstrate that you have understood the information you have been taught and that you are familiar with the knowledge required for the subject you are writing about. However, starting the writing process can be a challenging prospect, scary even. Further, developing your writing skills can be a fairly long process – it takes some practising. This chapter will provide guidance on different writing styles and on how to structure and plan your writing. It will also show how work is marked and how to respond to tutor feedback. Citing and referencing accurately to avoid plagiarism will be discussed and, finally, there will be some tips on how to overcome writer's block.

Writing styles

Within academic writing there are many different styles, depending on what is appropriate for the writing task. Cottrell (2008, p209) identifies four styles:

* descriptive;

* argumentative/analytical;

* evaluative/analytical;

* personal/experiential.

Descriptive writing is probably the easiest to start with as you simply describe the facts. You have to be precise and accurate in your description of what happened, what someone said (in reality or in a book), or description of key features. This type of writing is usually associated with 'report' writing. As a policing student you are likely to be familiar with writing reports, as you do this on a regular basis in, for instance, your notebook.

An example of descriptive writing would be:

> A student officer entering the Metropolitan Police Service must attend three, one-week 'Hydra' sessions at one of the training sites around London. The Hydra weeks are themed around Criminal Justice, Counter Terrorism and Public Protection. The activities are discussion based and students are given interactive assignments to complete.

However, although most essays contain some elements of descriptive writing, such as giving essential background information, you are also asked to be 'analytical'. An essay can be defined as 'a short piece of writing on a set topic' (Chambers and Northedge, 2008, p153) or, in other words: 'your opinion about a little bit of a subject, in which you use evidence to support your opinion' (Mounsey, 2002, p10). In an essay you need to examine the 'what, why, how' exactly, developing your ideas and opinions and demonstrating you can reason effectively, based on supporting evidence. Supporting evidence in this context means that your statements are backed up by what you have read in the literature, or other sources, on that subject. You need to show that you have looked at what the experts in the field say about the subject, in books or journals or sometimes on the internet, and use that to underpin your own thoughts and to base your argument on. The evidence consists of using quotes from the books/journals/internet, citing and referencing accurately what you have read. How to do that will be explained later in this chapter. Cottrell (2008) sums up that good argumentative writing:

- states your position or point of view;

- shows why it is valid by offering evidence or examples that support that position;

- considers a counter-argument, including evidence for the counter-argument – what your opponents would use to prove you are wrong;

- persuades a neutral party that your position is the stronger one.

The next stage of academic writing is also analytical but with an evaluative element, sometimes called 'synthesis' if strands are brought together. In evaluative writing you almost always consider two or more theories, ideas or beliefs that you 'compare and contrast'. By comparing them you bring out any similarities; by contrasting you focus on the differences. Next, you evaluate your findings: what are the strengths and limitations, and what are the implications of each theory, idea or belief? Based on this you make a judgement as to which theory, idea or belief you think is the preferred one, justifying your opinion. It is important that your essay is 'balanced', and that you write approximately the same number of words, using a similar pattern in your writing, for each theory. Although you are asked to be analytical and critical, this does not mean that you have to be completely negative. An essay is not the platform for having a go at your organisation or some theory, in other words a rant, just because you feel strongly about it.

Finally, sometimes you are asked to relate theory to your own practice. This is where you can use some examples from your own experience: personal or experiential writing. It is useful to reflect on whether your experience supports or contradicts theory and why. However, personal experience does not usually form the main part of your essay, although it can highlight certain aspects of a theory.

The conventions for academic writing are formal. You need to avoid using slang or abbreviations and explain the use of jargon as your tutors may not always be familiar with your practice. Writing is usually in the third person or passive voice: 'this essay will consider . . .', rather than 'in this essay, I will consider . . .', and it should use reasoning and be logically sequenced, taking an objective perspective. For all writing styles, make sure your use of grammar, punctuation and spelling is correct.

REFLECTIVE TASK

Look at the following extracts from two essays (the first one adapted from Roffey-Barentsen and Malthouse, 2009), titled 'An investigation into the role of Family Liaison Officers'. What are differences can you identify?

Essay 1

I would say that the role of the Family Liaison Officer is one of the most difficult and exacting positions within the police. They can be called whenever there is a need for a Family Liaison Officer and will be on call day and night on a rotational basis. I think it is important that they meet the diversity needs of the people in the community, especially ethnic minority groups. One thing they should know about for instance is the death rituals performed by other cultures. Obviously, every family will deal with their own grief in their own way and it will not lessen the family's sadness of losing a loved one but knowing about such stuff can only help and show respect. In this day and age it is important that we are seen to be doing the right thing.

Essay 2

This essay will investigate the role of Family Liaison Officers within the Police Service. First, it will identify elements of the role; second, it will discuss these elements, concluding that the role is a diverse and challenging one. Family Liaison Officers can be described as the go-betweens, or mediators, between the police and families who have been suddenly bereaved due to road deaths or murder. According to the National Policing Improvement Agency (2007, p92), their main role includes to 'analyse the needs, concerns and expectations of the family; work with them to comply with their right to receive all relevant information connected with the enquiry; and assist the investigation by gathering information and evidence from the family'. Family Liaison Officers should be tactful, sensitive and responsive to the needs of the families they work with, providing a two-way communication channel.

The role has been acknowledged as a pivotal one (Kent Police, 2009) in maintaining and establishing those meaningful links.

References:

Kent Police (2009) M96 Family Liaison Officers [online] Available at: www.kent.police.uk (accessed 2 February 2010).

National Policing Improvement Agency (2007) Road Death Investigation Manual [online] Available at www.acpo.police.uk (accessed 2 February 2010).

(The answer is given at the end of the chapter.)

Structuring your writing

The structure of an essay is almost as important as the content. Further, it will help you with your planning if you have a clear structure in mind for the essay. Although the topics you are writing about vary, the structure of a good essay stays the same. You should always have a:

- title/question;
- introduction;
- main body;
- conclusion;
- references/bibliography.

When examining the title of an essay, Bedford and Wilson (2006, p82) advise you to 'pick out the keywords'. Keywords will either be content-related, referring to the subject, or process-related, referring to what to do with the subject.

PRACTICAL TASK

Which words in the following essay title refer to content, and which to process?

   Evaluate the impact of the Stephen Lawrence Inquiry on police training

(The answer is given at the end of the chapter.)

Content words are specific to the module you are studying; however, process words may be used in any module. It is important to understand what these process words mean. Take time to consider the title carefully, making sure you address what it asks you to do. For instance, when asked to evaluate you should do more than just describe. You will be marked down for not answering the question, regardless of the time and effort you have put into writing a very detailed description. Table 3.1 shows the meanings of some process words.

Table 3.1 The meanings of process words

Process word	Meaning
Account for	Give reasons, explain why something happens
Analyse	Break topic into elements and examine each
Argue	Give reasons for and against, based on evidence
Assess	Make a judgement after considering in a balanced way the points for and against
Comment	State your opinions on a topic, supporting your views with evidence
Compare	Show similarities and differences
Contrast	Emphasise the differences between two or more things
Define	Give the precise meaning of something
Describe	Give a detailed account
Discuss	Consider different points of view
Evaluate	Consider and weigh the fors and againsts, making a judgement on which is preferable
Examine	Critically investigate
Explain	Make clear, giving reasons
To what extent	Consider how far something is true or not true
Illustrate	Use examples or diagrams to make clear and explicit
Interpret	Give the meaning of other material presented
Justify	Give reasons for decisions or conclusions
Outline	Give the main features
Review	Critically examine the subject
State	Say fully and clearly
Summarise	Give a concise account of the main points

Choose a subject, for instance 'Anti-social behaviour'. Add different process words and write down how they affect the approach to the essay. For example, what do you have to do for the essay to address 'Analyse anti-social behaviour'; 'Explain anti-social behaviour'; 'Justify anti-social behaviour'?

Each of these essays will look quite different; therefore, remember to keep your focus on the title throughout the essay, addressing the question.

It has been said that 'an essay is only as good as its introduction' (Mounsey, 2002, p34). You need to explain what the essay is going to do, what you are going to write about, and how you will support your argument, giving a brief outline of what you hope to demonstrate and summarising your conclusions. The first sentence is perhaps one of the most important in your essay, so keep it narrow and focused on the title or question. Consider starting with: 'This essay will argue/demonstrate/evaluate . . .'

Occasionally, essays start with a catchy quote or saying, to draw the reader in right from the start, creating interest and curiosity. However, make sure the quote you use is relevant to the subject and what you are saying about it. A loose quote, which does not make a point, detracts from your argument. Further, consider the appropriateness of quoting from a favourite childhood novel, if it is just there to amuse and invite a smile.

Look back at your previous essays. Do you have a preferred opening sentence?

After the introduction, the main body of the essay should be where you develop your argument by presenting your evidence (following the sequence as stated in the introduction). The main body consists of paragraphs, which break up the text to make it easier to read. The first sentence, sometimes called the 'topic sentence' (Cottrell, 2008, p192), introduces the main idea of the paragraph. Subsequent sentences develop this idea and the last sentence sums it up. You keep adding paragraphs until you have given sufficient evidence to support your argument. When adding paragraphs you must make sure that you appropriately link them – this is referred to as 'signposting'. Signposting ensures a fluency in your essay, which makes it easier for the reader to follow your line of reasoning and argument. The following words are commonly used to link paragraphs:

Furthermore, moreover, in other words, firstly, secondly, finally, conversely, on the other hand, by contrast, therefore, as a result, to summarise, etc.

The conclusion of your essay should summarise your argument, drawing only from the evidence you have presented, linking it to the title. It is important that you should not introduce any new material or evidence at this stage. In some way, the conclusion revisits the introduction. The two should be strongly connected to provide a 'rounded' essay.

Finally, at the end of your essay, provide a reference list of all the evidence (books, journals, internet, etc.) you have quoted from or referred to in your writing (see section on 'Citing and referencing', pages 50–2). Sometimes you may also be asked to provide a 'bibliography', which includes material you have used to inform yourself but did not refer to in the essay. Make sure to check with your tutor whether to include a reference list and/or bibliography.

Planning your writing

One of the first things you need to find out, either from a handbook or from your tutor, is the word count for the work. How flexible this is depends on your university; some allow you to be either 10 per cent under or over the word count. Direct quotes do not usually form part of the word count, to avoid excessive citing, but you will need to confirm this with your tutor.

Although some students try putting off the idea of writing for as long as possible, general advice is to give yourself plenty of time, especially if work for different modules is due in on the same submission date. Although you may not start the writing until the end of the taught sessions of the module, it will be helpful to consider the essay or assignment for that module early on, as this will help you with your responses to the reading: what is going to be useful and what is not, and allowing you to follow up references in good time.

Writing an essay does not simply happen. Unfortunately, you cannot expect to sit yourself at your computer the night before the submission date and write a good piece of work. The writing needs to be planned carefully. As a start, consider the planning procedure in Table 3.2.

Marking and tutor feedback

After submitting their work, students are usually very eager to find out their results. In a way, you can anticipate your mark by checking your work against the marking criteria and assessment descriptors for the appropriate level that are used by the tutors (the criteria are stated in the handbook or available from your tutor). In general, lower marks are awarded to essays that lack structure, provide little evidence of wider reading to support the argument and are mostly descriptive in nature. Higher marks are given to essays that have a clear structure, develop an argument based on appropriate evidence and take a critical, analytical approach. The highest marks are for essays that reveal a sound understanding of the topic and its wider issues and implications, beyond the subject area, supported by extensive reading.

Marking on a degree programme, for each piece of work, is usually in percentages that relate to degree classifications (see box below).

Alternatively, the piece may be awarded a pass, merit or distinction. Find out which awarding system is used by your college or university, so you are more prepared for what you are aiming for.

Table 3.2 Essay planning procedure

	Procedure	Description
1	Essay title	Examine and analyse the title or essay question, clarifying the task.
2	Gathering information	Write down your ideas for the essay and start selecting appropriate material from the literature, such as books, journals, internet, articles, reports, etc. Be careful to record in detail where you found the information, in case you want to go back to it, or in case you want to use it directly in your writing. You can either keep these notes in alphabetical order by author, or you can arrange them in themes, or even colour-code them.
3	Organise your material and reflect	Consider your notes, cluster ideas and consider a sequence for these ideas. Reflect on your findings and opinions. Keep in mind where you want to go, referring back to the title. Is the gathered evidence sufficient or do you need to go back to the sources?
4	Plan first draft	Outline your first draft, allocating word counts to different parts of the essay. Check there is logical reasoning behind your argument, based on relevant evidence. If possible, discuss the draft with your tutor. Tutors are not always allowed to 'pre-mark' full assignments or essays, but can give you feedback on work in progress. Discussing your draft with a peer or colleague also helps you to clarify your ideas. If necessary, repeat this process for subsequent drafts.
5	Final draft	Respond to the feedback given, either by tutor or peer, revising the draft. Check your English, and make sure all citing and referencing is accurate. Do a final word count. Check you have met the required format of presentation for the assignment or essay (margin, line-spacing, etc.). Proof-read the final draft, or ask someone else to do this for you. Then you're ready to: SUBMIT!

REFLECTIVE TASK

Thinking back on your previous essays, how did you plan these, and how did you ensure that they were completed?

Percentage	Class
70+	First
60–69	Second (upper division)
50–59	Second (lower division)
40–49	Third
0–39	Refer

When getting work back, it is tempting to take a quick look at the grade before putting it away somewhere, especially if you are disappointed with the result, feeling that the time and effort you have put into it are not reflected by the mark. Although the mark or grade is an indication of the level of that particular essay or assignment, it is just that, not a personal attack. For all students, regardless of the grade, it is more important to read the feedback and comments from your tutor. Your main focus has to be: how can I improve? Your tutor may have identified 'areas for improvement' on the marking sheet, which can help you to construct an 'action plan' for the next essay or assignment. If not, look at all comments carefully, taking time to understand them fully. Consider arranging a tutorial with your tutor if comments are not clear. Do not feel embarrassed; the writing process is a hard one, and you can only improve by discussing your work with your tutor and responding to his or her feedback.

PRACTICAL TASK

Draw up an action plan from the following tutor feedback.

> *You have made a good start on identifying the individual elements of the topic, showing some analysis. There is evidence of relevant wider reading, but be careful not to rely overly on one source. You demonstrate appropriate subject knowledge and make some interesting and accurate observations. Your argument is logically sequenced, but consider more use of signposting to improve the flow. Further, make sure you proof-read your work beforehand as there are some spelling errors. Overall, a good effort.*

(The answer is given at the end of the chapter.)

Citing and referencing

To demonstrate evidence of your wider reading, supporting your arguments, you have to cite and reference your sources accurately.

The 'citing' happens in the text, as you make use of direct quotes or refer to someone's writing. The 'referencing' is at the end, listing your sources. Appropriate wider reading strengthens your writing, and therefore your marks, as it demonstrates to your tutors that you are familiar with relevant knowledge regarding the subject. Basing your opinions and arguments on established authors increases the credibility of your work. Tutors, or anyone else who is reading your work, should be able to locate your source easily, not just to check up, but also to use as a starting point for further reading. Although there are different systems for citing and referencing, such as author-date systems or numerical ones using footnotes, the one explained further here is the commonly used Harvard system. However, do check with your tutors which system you should adopt.

Table 3.3 shows some guidelines to citing and referencing, giving examples of what the quotes/citations look like in the main body of your work and in the reference list at the end of your work.

Table 3.3 Citing and referencing

In the main body of the work	In the reference list
Short quotation from a book: 2 or 3 lines set in quotation marks, listing author, date and page number, e.g. Madsen states that 'citizen-focused policing is a branch of the government's wider neighbourhood policing policy' (2007, p50).	Author, initial, date of publication, title of work, place of publishing, publisher, e.g. Madsen, S. (2007) *Practical Skills for Police Community Support Officers*. Exeter: Learning Matters.
Longer quotation from book: quotation marks not required, indented from text, e.g. When discussing citizen-focused policing Madsen states that: *citizen-focused policing is a branch of the government's wider neighbourhood policing policy. It is defined as a way of working in which an in-depth understanding of the needs of individuals and local communities is routinely reflected in day-to-day decision making and service delivery.* (Madsen, 2007, p50)	Madsen, S (2007) *Practical Skills for Police Community Support Officers*. Exeter: Learning Matters.
Paraphrasing what an author says, e.g. As argued by Merritt (2007), it appears that the concept of fundamental human rights is not always easy to grasp.	Merritt, J (2007) *Law for Student Police Officers*. Exeter: Learning Matters.
Citation from a book edited by someone else, e.g. Madsen (2007) explains that the role of police constables can be challenging as well as rewarding	Madsen, S (ed.) (2007) *Practical Policing Skills for Student Officers*. Exeter: Learning Matters.
Citation from journal article, e.g. Cohen (1997) suggests that Gardner's Multiple Intelligences can be used with learners to explore their assumptions about learning.	Author, initial, date, title of article, journal (italics), volume, page, e.g. Cohen, LR (1997) I ain't so smart and you ain't so dumb: personal reassessment in transformative learning. *New Directions for Adult and Continuing Education*, 74: 61–8.
Quote from internet (author known), e.g. 'Most of the examples in *Cite them right* are given in an author-date referencing style commonly known as Harvard style' (Pears and Shields, 2008).	Pears, R and Shields, G (2008) *Cite them right* [online]. Available at www.citethemright.co.uk (accessed 27 August 2009).
Quote from internet (author unknown), e.g. 'The "Harvard Style" is a standard format to create your bibliography references in for your essays' (Neilstoolbox.com, 2009)	Neilstoolbox.com (2009) *In the Toolbox* [online]. Available at www.neilstoolbox.com/ (accessed 19 July 2009).

Table 3.3 Continued

In the main body of the work	In the reference list
Quote from 3 or more authors: Use first author followed by 'et al.', e.g. Malthouse et al. state that 'interactive exercises are an important part of the Police recruitment process' (2009, p2).	List all authors, e.g. Malthouse, R, Kennard, P and Roffey-Barentsen, J (2009) *Interactive Exercises for the Police Recruit Assessment Process.* Exeter: Learning Matters.
Secondary referencing, quoting from a book citing another author, e.g. Graef (1990), cited in Merritt (2007, p80) found that some officers considered anything to do with the community is not 'macho'.	If you have read Merritt only, then you can only reference Merritt: Merritt, J (2007) *Law for Student Police Officers.* Exeter: Learning Matters. Do not include full references to Graef unless you have read his work yourself. Ideally, read both.
Quote from government publications, e.g. 'In recent years there have been significant changes in the way leadership is exercised at national level in policing' (Home Office, 2008, p65)	Home Office (2008) *From the Neighbourhood to the National: Policing our Communities Together* [online]. Available at http://police.homeoffice.gov.uk/publications/ (accessed 2 July 2009).
Ibid.: short for ibidem (Latin for 'in the same place'), is used to save writing the details of a source every time it is used. This means the reader has to trace the reference back to where it was used previously (which can be frustrating for the reader)	Source already referenced as it was used before.

Plagiarism

Plagiarism is when you present other people's work or ideas as your own, without acknowledging them. This can be written work, but also visual or electronic material. In the most obvious cases, whole essays or major parts thereof are copied and pasted from the internet or other source. However, the more common cases of plagiarism are often less intentional, such as omitting quotation marks, paraphrasing that is too close to the original, or 'borrowed' sentences that are not acknowledged. Colleges and universities routinely check for plagiarism, as it is considered a very serious offence. When accused of plagiarism, the consequences are severe. In the worst cases, the students will be withdrawn from the course; in other cases marks will be reduced (affecting the overall grade). Therefore, be precise and accurate in your citing and referencing (including material from the internet).

PRACTICAL TASK

Given the following original text, are the subsequent examples plagiarised?

Whereas the powers to direct people to leave land can be exercised by the senior police officer present at the scene, the power under s .63 is restricted to an officer of at least superintendent rank. The officer must have a reasonable belief that one of the circumstances set out in s. 63(2) applies in respect of any land in the open air. Those circumstances are that:

- *at least two people are making preparations for the holding of a relevant gathering; or*

- *at least ten people are waiting for such a gathering to begin or are attending such a gathering which is in progress.*

(Hutton and McKinnon, 2008, p373)

Example 1

Only a superintendent can ask people to leave land in the open air. The officer must believe that:

(a) at least two people are making preparations for the holding of a gathering; or

(b) at least ten people are attending or waiting to begin such a gathering.

Example 2

Asking people to leave a field can only be done by a superintendent. It applies when there are either more than two people organising the event, or more than ten people taking part.

Example 3

Hutton and McKinnon (2008) state: Whereas the powers to direct people to leave land can be exercised by the senior police officer present at the scene, the power under s .63 is restricted to an officer of at least superintendent rank.

(The answer is given at the end of the chapter.)

Writer's block

It happens to everybody at some point; you stare at a blank screen, not knowing where to start, or are stuck on a paragraph. Here are some suggestions that might help.

- Relax for a while, to take your (conscious) mind off the work.

- Try brainstorming.

- Draw a mind map; some software packages allow you to do this on a computer, using different colours, fonts, etc.

- Explain your work to someone else; talk it through.

- Remember you are working on a draft, not perfection.

- Just start – give it a go. It is easier to develop something once you have started than from nothing.

C H A P T E R   S U M M A R Y

In this chapter we have looked at four different writing styles and have examined the structure and planning of an essay or assignment. How to recognise allocation of marks/grades for a piece of writing has been explained and we have shown you how to respond constructively to tutor feedback. Finally, the importance of citing and referencing correctly has been stressed and we have suggested some ways of overcoming writer's block.

Answers to tasks

Essay comparison (pages 44–5)

Essay 1 is entirely descriptive, based on the writer's own opinion ('I would say', 'I think'). It is written in the first person ('I') and makes extensive use of everyday language ('obviously', 'in this day and age'), including slang ('stuff').

Essay 2 is analytical and clear in its approach; it tells exactly what the essay will cover. There is evidence of wider reading, in the use of citing and referencing, to support the argument. It is written in the third person ('This essay will') and uses a more formal language.

Although Essay 1 may be easy to read and appears to be written with some passion, Essay 2 is the more academic one, and is in a style more appropriate for your study.

Essay title (page 46)

Stephen Lawrence Inquiry refers to content; evaluate to process.

Action plan (page 50)

1. Be more detailed in the analysis, break the topic down in even smaller chunks and take a critical look, making links to the reading, and commenting on arguments for and against.

2. Do more reading, and vary the sources (books, journals, internet) to demonstrate all-round, in-depth knowledge of the subject.

3. Make it easier for the reader to follow the writing by linking the paragraphs a bit more (rather than a 'shopping list').

4. Spell-check! Also check for words that are spelled correctly but have an alternative meaning that is unsuitable for the context.

Plagiarism (page 53)

- Example 1, although paraphrased, is in places very close to the original text and therefore needs further 'putting into own words' or appropriate referencing.

- Example 2 is sufficiently paraphrased.

- Example 3, although the authors are mentioned, needs quotation marks for the direct quote. Therefore, the example will be considered as having been plagiarised.

Bedford, D and Wilson, E (2006) *Study Skills for Foundation Degrees*. London: David Fulton Publishers.

Chambers, E and Northedge, A (2008) *The Arts Good Study Guide*. Milton Keynes: The Open University.

Cottrell, S (2008) *The Study Skills Handbook*. Basingstoke: Palgrave Macmillan.

Hutton, G and McKinnon, G (2008) *Blackstone's Police Manual: Volume 4, General Police Duties*, 11th edition. Oxford: Oxford University Press.

Mounsey, C (2002) *Essays and Dissertations*. Oxford: Oxford University Press.

Roffey-Barentsen, J and Malthouse, R (2009) *Reflective Practice in the Lifelong Learning Sector*. Exeter: Learning Matters.

To check your work for plagiarism, try:

http://turnitin.com (Turn it in online; your college or university may subscribe to this site)

www.neilstoolbox.com (also contains tools for referencing and writing clarity, as well as for avoiding plagiarism)

For help in referencing, try:

www.citethemright.co.uk (Cite them right claims to be 'the essential referencing guide')

4 Critical and analytical thinking skills

LINKS TO STANDARDS

This chapter provides opportunities for links with the following Skills for Justice, National Occupational Standards (NOS) for Policing and Law Enforcement 2008.

AB1.1   Communicate effectively with people
AE1.1   Maintain and develop your own knowledge and competence

Introduction

Being able to think critically and analytically is a skill that you need to apply throughout your academic and professional career. First, when listening to lectures or other people, or when reading a report, article or textbook, you need to adopt a challenging approach, questioning what has been presented to you, and not take what you hear or read for granted. You need to be able to identify the strengths and weaknesses in an argument and feel confident to query statements that are presented as evidence or facts.

Second, when constructing your own argument, either in writing or, for instance, in a presentation, you need to ensure that others consider your decisions and judgements to be secure and verified. When starting their university courses, many students lack this critical, analytical approach, which is often reflected in the feedback they receive from their tutors, such as: 'This assignment would benefit from a more critical approach.' To enable you to enhance those skills, this chapter discusses:

- what is meant by critical thinking;
- how to identify and analyse an argument;
- flaws in arguments;
- how to evaluate the evidence.

What is critical thinking?

Critical thinking is not a new concept. In the 1930s Dewey defined it as 'active, persistent, and careful consideration of any belief or supposed form of knowledge in the light of the grounds that support it and the further conclusions to which it tends' (1933, p118). More recently, Judge et al. put it succinctly as 'a questioning, challenging approach to knowledge and perceived wisdom which involves examining ideas and information from an objective position and then questioning this information in the light of our own values, attitudes and personal philosophy' (2009, p1). Cottrell (2005, p2) very clearly identifies the range of skills and attitudes that constitute critical thinking:

- identifying other people's positions, arguments and conclusions;
- evaluating the evidence for alternative points of view;
- weighing up opposing arguments and evidence fairly;
- being able to read between the lines, seeing behind surfaces, and identifying false or unfair assumptions;
- recognising techniques used to make certain positions more appealing than others, such as false logic and persuasive devices;
- reflecting on issues in a structured way, bringing logic and insight to bear;
- drawing conclusions about whether arguments are valid and justifiable, based on good evidence and sensible assumptions;
- presenting a point of view in a structured, clear, well-reasoned way that convinces others.

Critical thinking skills are closely related to problem-solving skills. Employers often test new applicants on these skills, making use of the Watson-Glaser Critical Thinking Appraisal (Glaser, 1941), which measures the ability to draw inferences, recognise assumptions, draw conclusions, interpret data and evaluate arguments, or the Cornell Critical Thinking Test, devised by Ennis (1964).

Identifying and analysing an argument

In everyday life, an argument is a disagreement or a dispute. In the worst scenario, what started as a mere argument between people can escalate into a fight, requiring police assistance. However, in the academic world, an argument can be described as an attempt to persuade others (of the validity of the conclusion), by offering at least one reason that supports that conclusion. This means that an argument starts with an issue, which, followed by a line of thinking or reasoning, leads to a conclusion. So, to identify the argument, you have to first find the issue and conclusion of what you have heard or read and also the reasons that led to that conclusion.

Identifying the issue can be a simple process. Sometimes the author or speaker raises the issue explicitly in the title or opening paragraph of their essay or speech, for instance:

- *Safer neighbourhoods; is it a matter of police visibility?*

- *Should speed limits be lowered in inner city areas?*

- *Is it right that offenders are offered education?*

However, the issue is not always so easy to identify. Sometimes it is inferred, which means you have to find a question that is addressed throughout the essay. The best way to do this is by looking at the conclusion. What does the author try to convey; what is his or her message? Although most of the time you'll find the conclusion at the end of the essay, this is not always the case. The next place to look is at the beginning, as some authors like to begin an essay with a statement of purpose, explaining what they are trying to prove. It is helpful to look for clue words as they usually lead to what the author is trying to persuade you of. Clue words include:

> *therefore, so, thus, in consequence, as a result, hence, shows that, indicates that, proves that.*

Once you have established what the conclusion is and what the issue was in the first place, you can look for the reasons the author gives in order to convince you that the conclusion made is the 'right' one. The reasons support the conclusion. There must be at least one reason for there to be an argument; however, most of the time there are more.

PRACTICAL TASK

Which of the following examples are arguments?

1. More and more elderly people are scared in their own homes. Burglaries in London are up by 5 per cent. A minimum sentence of three years' custody on a third conviction for domestic burglary has recently been introduced.

2. Any amount of alcohol affects your ability to drive. There is no foolproof way of drinking and staying under the limit, or of knowing how much an individual person can drink and still drive safely. So the only safe option is not to drink alcohol if you plan to drive.

3. Alternative measures to discourage young people from taking drugs need to be introduced. Many young people use recreational drugs. A reclassification of drugs has had no effect on the number of young people taking drugs.

(The answers are given at the end of the chapter.)

Remember, an argument has to be persuasive. Sometimes, what may look like an argument is nothing more than an explanation. Consider the following example:

> The 'early shift' starts at 6.00 a.m. Officers come in 15 minutes earlier. Therefore, the canteen opens at 5.45 a.m.

Although it appears that the example is an argument, as there are two reasons supporting a conclusion, it is not persuasive. It is just an explanation of why the canteen opens at 5.45 a.m. Of course, explanations, or specific examples, are often used to support the conclusion. It is up to you to make a judgement as to whether or not they provide such support.

What about the following example; is this an argument?

> Police Officers must have good communication skills. Their patience is often tested. Also, it helps to have a sense of humour. Therefore, to become a Police Officer, you must be patient, have good communication skills and have a healthy sense of humour.

Again, this statement looks like an argument. However, what appears to be the conclusion is a summary of what has been stated before. The conclusion is not based on reasoning; therefore, this is not an example of an argument.

In life, we are surrounded by attempts to persuade us. Just think of politics, the media or advertising. You have to decide which (attempts) to accept and which to reject, and why you have made these decisions. Therefore, when reading a text, or listening to a speech or lecture, it is useful to ask yourself the following questions.

- Does the evidence support the conclusions; is it relevant and adequate?

- Based on the line of reasoning, would I come to the same conclusions?

PRACTICAL TASK

- *Write an argument on an issue you feel strongly in favour of, including a conclusion and line of reasoning to support that conclusion.*

- *Now take the opposite view, writing an argument against that same issue.*

- *Reflect: how relevant and adequate was your line of reasoning in the first task? Have you persuaded yourself that the second viewpoint is better?*

Referring to the task above, you probably found it easier to write an argument on an issue you feel strongly in favour of, rather than taking the opposite view. Further to that, it is unlikely that you persuaded yourself that the opposite view is the better one. If you recognise this in your own thinking, it is probably safe to assume that authors may also be influenced by certain angles. It is therefore good practice to check the background and credibility of the author. Does he or she have a political stance? What hidden agendas might the author have; what does he or she hope to gain through writing this piece? Further, consider if any information might be missing – information that could paint a different picture. Who might disagree with the author? Therefore, before making a judgement you need to evaluate carefully the evidence presented to you.

Evaluating the evidence

When evaluating the evidence there a number of areas to consider. As discussed above, you first look at the author: who they are, what their background is, including their knowledge of the subject. Second, you look at the piece of writing itself: are there any ambiguities or inconsistencies; does the author base the evidence on facts or opinion; can you detect any flaws or errors in logic?

Specialist knowledge

The first area to check is the author's specialist knowledge or expertise. Are they an expert in their field? If they lack expertise, arguably, their credibility would be weakened. For example, someone who does not know the rules, regulations and terminology used in cricket may not recognise a Chinese cut (an inside edge that misses hitting the stumps by a few centimetres), and would therefore probably not comment on it. After all, it is difficult to interpret evidence accurately if you lack specialist knowledge. But how would you know if the author is an expert? To find out, it is useful to investigate if they have published any other books or articles in journals; or do other authors, who have written on the same subject, refer to them in their publications (check the references in other authors' books!). How many times a name appears is usually a good indication of whether you are dealing with an expert or a novice in the field. However, this does not mean that a novice writer cannot be very experienced. Alternatively, if you find out that the author is an established expert, this doesn't mean you can't be critical in your approach, questioning the reasoning used and considering alternative views.

Bias and hidden agendas

Browne and Keeley (2007, p112) point out that factors such as personal needs, prior expectations, general beliefs, attitudes, values, theories and ideologies can subconsciously or deliberately influence how evidence is reported. As well as being aware of your own bias and prejudices, which may interfere with how you judge the presented evidence, you also have to consider bias and subjectivity in the author. For instance, if the Chief Constable is asked whether cuts in policing, proposed by the Home Office, are welcome, the answer would probably be 'no', followed by a list of examples of how cuts would negatively affect police performance and national security. The reasoning may sound convincing but is it an unbiased, objective view? Although objectivity is at the heart of critical thinking, it is likely that there are some subjective elements or statements in the text that you are reading. There could be hidden or underlying assumptions; what does the author want you to take for granted?

Further, when reading reports or statements and so on, it is useful for policing students and officers to consider the reliability of the author. Have they lied in the past; is there anything at stake; is there anything to gain by not telling the (entire) truth? With witness accounts you have to query whether the witness was in a position to see what happened themselves; was their view obscured; did they assume things happened, jumping to conclusions?

Ambiguity (equivocation)

When evaluating the evidence presented, carefully look at the use of language. On occasion language can be ambiguous and interpreted in more than one way. For instance, when referring to 'crime', what is meant? When talking to someone you can ask them to explain themselves; however, in a written text it may take time to work out what is meant by careful and close reading. Keep asking if any other interpretation is possible, 'what could be meant' and 'what it means in this context'. Browne and Keeley (2007) advise that you cannot evaluate an essay until you know the communicator's intended meaning of key terms and phrases, as well as alternative meanings.

Ambiguity is often intended, especially if certain meanings have emotive connotations. You are more likely to accept the author's way of thinking if he or she can play on your emotions. The emotional impact is quite intentional and is carefully planned by the authors.

Inconsistency

Next, check for consistency. This means that you consider all parts of the line of reasoning that led to the conclusion. Are there any parts that contradict or undermine the main message? If claims are contradictory, that means at least one of them must be false. Therefore, an argument that rests on contradictory claims must rest on at least one false claim, and arguments that rest on false claims prove nothing. To dismiss the argument, you don't even have to know which of the two contradicting claims is the false one. As stated by Cottrell, 'Inconsistencies make an argument hard to follow, leaving the audience uncertain about what the author is trying to persuade them to believe' (2005, p65). Therefore, inconsistencies in a text obliterate its credibility and persuasive powers, for example:

> Life is precious and can't be given back. Punishment for taking a life should be severe. Therefore, bring back the death penalty.

Fact or opinion?

An opinion is a personal point of view or a belief, not based on proof or evidence. It doesn't carry much power to persuade; after all, what does one person's opinion matter? Facts, on the other hand, can be checked against evidence and proven to be true, thereby adding weight to the argument. Therefore, in their efforts to convince you to accept their conclusions, authors often make factual claims. They present something as fact, thereby discouraging you from questioning what they have said. However, when applying your critical thinking skills, your response should be 'why should I believe that', 'what is the evidence', 'how strong is the evidence'?

One tool often used as factual evidence is 'statistics'. The numbers appear scientific and can come across as very convincing. However, they do not always provide the proof the author claims to provide. You may have heard of the saying 'There are three kinds of lies: lies, damned lies and statistics.' You have to be very careful how to interpret statistical evidence. Question who or what organisation is behind the statistics, and what is their mission.

PRACTICAL TASK

How would you question the following claim?

In the last year crime figures have dropped by 10 per cent.

Although the sentence in the above task sounds like a positive development, being critical means asking questions like those following.

- What is meant by crime? It could be that certain acts, previously considered to be a crime, are now no longer so.

- Has there been a drop in reported crime, which means it is still going on but we don't know about it?

- What does 10 per cent mean; is it likely to have an impact? Is 10 per cent the average drop in crime figures, which means some might actually have gone up?

- Who made the claim; was it the Home Office or a local newspaper?

- Was the drop in crime nationwide or in a shopping centre?

- How recent is the claim and therefore the statistics? Always look for up-to-date figures and data.

- Are there other reports that support the claim or claim other statistics?

The main thing is that you don't just accept what you have been told; question it!

Logical fallacies

Logical fallacies are common errors of reasoning. This means that the reasons provided do not prove the argument's conclusion. Browne and Keeley (2007, p85) describe a fallacy as 'a reasoning "trick" that an author might use while trying to persuade you to accept a conclusion'. It is helpful to recognise them in an argument as they immediately make you query the conclusion.

Some of the most common 'tricks' are listed below (alphabetically).

Ad hominem

'Ad hominem' is the Latin phrase for 'against the man' or 'against the person'. It is most commonly used to attack the person offering an argument rather than the argument itself. This is often used in politics, where politicians are attacked on their character, background, interests, personal circumstances, etc., rather than on the policy or strategy they support. The attention is shifted away from the argument to the person. Or, as

Browne and Keeley put it: 'It is attacking the messenger instead of addressing the message' (2007, p85).

Examples of this fallacy can be found regularly in the media, especially with regard to politicians, whose personal lives often attract more attention than their policies.

Appeal to authority
This is an argument that tries to establish its conclusion by citing a perceived authority who claims that the conclusion is true.

Appeals to authority are nearly always fallacious. Just because someone says that something is true, this doesn't prove that it *is* true; no matter how well respected someone is, it is possible that they are wrong on this occasion. The worst kind is 'appeal to questionable authority', where the alleged authority isn't an authority on the subject matter in question. Alleged authorities speaking outside their area of expertise should not be trusted without further investigation. Be particularly careful when citing an internet site as your authority. An official-sounding organisation, association, or even university, may be misleading you, for example:

> *Nuclear power stations are dangerous and should be closed; my inspector says so.*

Before you can support the conclusion that nuclear power stations should be closed, you need to consider the evidence that the authority, in this case the inspector, is using to make the judgement. Unless the inspector is a nuclear scientist, with support for the claim, the reason 'because the inspector says so' is a fallacy.

Appeal to history or antiquity
Appeal to history or antiquity assumes that older ideas are best; because something has been done in a particular way in the past, it ought to be done that way in the future. This is also known as the appeal to tradition. However, the way that things have always been done is not necessarily the best way to do them now. Old ideas can be good or bad, just as new ideas can be good or bad. You can't learn anything about the truth of an idea just by looking at how old it is.

Appeal to ignorance
In an appeal to ignorance the arguer wants you to accept a conclusion on the grounds that there isn't any other evidence available, for example:

> *Scientific studies so far have not proven that individual tutorials are beneficial to students on a policing degree. Therefore, individual tutorials are not beneficial.*

Appeal to popularity (ad populum)
Appeals to popularity argue that, because lots of people believe something, it must be true. This is of course not always the case. Even ideas that are widely accepted can be false. Closely related to this is the 'bandwagon fallacy', which places an emphasis on more current ideas and trends. As before, because of their growing popularity, ideas are considered to be true, for example:

> *Everyone knows that only gay people and drug users can get Aids.*

Circular argument or begging the question

An argument is circular if its conclusion is also one of its reasons; if it assumes (either explicitly or not) what it is trying to prove. Arguments like these won't achieve anything. If you accept the reasons to be true, you already accept the argument's conclusion, so the argument can't have convinced you. If you reject the argument's conclusion, you should also reject at least one of its reasons (the one that is the same as its conclusion), and so you should reject the argument as a whole. In either case, the argument has accomplished nothing, for example:

> If the possession of a weapon wasn't illegal, it would not be forbidden by the law.

Confusing necessary and sufficient conditions

Necessary conditions are ones that must be met, otherwise an event can't happen. For example, a necessary condition of you being awarded your (Foundation) Degree in Policing is that you enrol on the course. If you don't, you cannot be awarded the degree.

If met, sufficient conditions guarantee that an event will happen. It is impossible for an event not to happen if the sufficient conditions for it are met. For example, a sufficient condition of you being awarded your degree is that you pass all the assignments. You cannot fail to be awarded your degree if you meet that condition.

Arguments that confuse necessary and sufficient conditions fail to prove their conclusions, for example:

> Students who don't read around the subject they're studying always fail their assignment. I've read a lot, so my assignment will pass.

Not having read around the subject may be a sufficient condition for failing an assignment, but it isn't a necessary condition. Even if you have read around the subject, there may be other reasons why you fail an assignment, for instance by not adopting a critical approach!

Correlation not causation

This fallacy is committed when it is argued that, just because there is a correlation between two events, they are associated, and one must be caused by the other. However, although it is true that the cause comes before the event, there could be many other things happening before the event, most of which will not be causal but mere coincidences. It is important to consider other possible explanations before concluding that one thing must have caused the other. Closely related to this is the fallacy of not recognising when something is caused by something else, which is called neglect of a cause, for example:

> Since the appointment of the extra officers, crime figures have risen. They are obviously not doing their job properly.

In this example you cannot argue that crime rates have gone up because of the extra officers. You need to consider other explanations, such as a growth in population, a drop in the number of security guards employed by shops, etc.

Generalisation

The fallacy 'generalisation' is committed when a sweeping statement is made, coming to a conclusion, although the evidence provided is not sufficient to support the conclusion, for example:

> All police officers I spoke to at a training centre last week had started their career either as a PCSO or as a Special. Therefore, you have to be a PCSO or Special before you can apply to become a police officer.

As you'll agree, this conclusion is not based on a sufficient number of cases. Furthermore, the cases must be representative.

Non sequitur

This is the Latin term for 'doesn't follow'. It means that reasons given in an argument do not necessarily lead to the conclusion. This fallacy is related to the 'correlation not causation' one.

Post hoc ergo propter hoc

This fallacy, which means in Latin 'after this, therefore because of this', is related to the 'correlation not causation' fallacy. It assumes that, because one event preceded another, it was the cause of it.

Red herring

This is a fallacy of distraction, which is committed when a listener attempts to divert an arguer from the argument by introducing another topic. An appeal to pity is often used to provide that distraction, for example:

> That homeless person may have stolen from the shop, but look at that poor, thin, mangy greyhound; do you think it has fleas?

Slippery slope

The slippery slope is a fallacy in which one set of events is shown to lead inevitably to another, without providing evidence for this inevitability. Sometimes, there are a number of steps or gradations between one event and the one in question, without any explanation or reasons why those steps have happened.

This sort of 'reasoning' is fallacious because there is no evidence to prove that one event must inevitably follow from another without an argument for such a claim, for example:

> The age limit of young people buying alcohol should not be reduced. Before we know it toddlers will be found drunk in the playground.

Straw man

As stated by Browne and Keeley (2007), the straw man, or straw person, fallacy is committed when the opponent's point of view is distorted, so that it is easy to attack; thus the writer is attacking a point of view that doesn't really exist. Unfortunately, adopting this strategy means that only the misrepresentation of the position is attacked; the real position is left untouched, for example:

> Animal activists want us to eat beans and roots and wear grass skirts.

Tu quoque

Pronounced 'too kwoh kwe', this is Latin for 'you too'. This fallacy justifies your wrongdoing because other people do it as well. In other words, because someone or everyone else does something, it's okay for you to do it as well, for example:

> It's ok to park on the yellow zigzag line; everyone else does it.

However, as you know, two wrongs don't make a right!

Weak analogy

Arguments by analogy rest on a comparison between two cases. The argument is only as strong as that comparison. The more similar the cases are, the stronger the argument. The weak analogy fallacy, or 'false analogy', is committed when there are significant dissimilarities between the two cases.

PRACTICAL TASK

Read the following passage; which fallacies can you detect?

> *The feminist argument that pornography is harmful has no merit and should not be discussed in college courses. I read 'Playboy' magazine, and I don't see how it could be harmful. Feminists might criticise me for looking at porn, but they shouldn't talk; they obviously look at it, too, or they couldn't criticise it. Many important people, including the presidents, writers and entertainers who have been interviewed by the magazine and the women who pose in it, apparently agree. Scientific studies so far have not proved that pornography is harmful, so it must not be harmful. Feminists should take a lesson from my parents – they don't like loud music and won't have it in their houses, but they don't go around saying it's harmful to everyone or trying to prevent others from listening to it. Ever since feminists began attacking our popular culture, the moral foundation of our society has been weakened; the divorce rate, for example, continues to rise. If feminists would just cease their hysterical opposition to sex, perhaps relationships in our society would improve. If feminists insist, instead, on banning porn, large numbers of women will be jobless and will have to work as prostitutes to support themselves. In light of these consequences, feminists shouldn't be surprised if their protests are met with violence. Truly, the feminist argument is baseless.*

(from www.unc.edu/depts/wcweb/handouts/fallacyargument.htm)

(The answer is given at the end of the chapter.)

Applying critical thinking to your own work

Now that you can recognise fallacies in other people's writing (or speeches), take a critical look at your own writing. When constructing an argument, try to convince others of your view and conclusion by offering appropriate, logical reasoning rather than falling into the trap of using common fallacies. To achieve this, first take a step back from your work, then pretend you disagree with the conclusion. If you were the opposition, where could you see the gaps in the reasoning – which elements of the argument seem weak? If you can identify those, so can your tutor, colleague or opponent. List all reasons leading to your conclusion – are they adequate, sufficient? If not, how can you strengthen them? Be especially careful when using general statements such as 'all', 'every', 'never' and 'always'; do you really have the evidence to make such claims? Further, make sure you keep your argument factual, not launching a personal attack on someone's character. Finally, when looking back at work you have done before, have you used any fallacies? At this stage of your studies you may 'appeal to authority' in an attempt to boost credibility, or rely on 'ad populum' statements as they seem a safe option ('everybody knows that').

Looking at your own work in this critical way allows you to substantiate your evidence (if required), writing in a convincing, persuasive manner. This, of course, will have a positive impact on your grades.

C H A P T E R   S U M M A R Y

In this chapter we have examined a definition of critical thinking and the elements that constitute an 'argument'. We have described how to evaluate evidence presented in an argument and have shown you how to recognise some common logical fallacies. Finally, we have shown how to apply critical thinking to your own work.

Answers to tasks

Identifying arguments (page 58)

1. This is not an argument. These are just three sentences; none of them would work as a conclusion, drawn from the other two.

2. This is an argument. The third sentence is the conclusion, supported by reasons given in the first and second sentences.

3. This is an argument. The first sentence is the conclusion drawn from the second and third sentences.

Identifying fallacies (page 66)

On the left of the following table are the fallacious arguments; the explanation of them is on the right.

Fallacious argument	Explanation
The feminist argument that pornography is harmful has no merit and should not be discussed in college courses.	This is the overall conclusion. 'Should not be discussed in college courses' = unrelated to the arguments that follow, so this is missing the point.
I read 'Playboy' magazine, and I don't see how it could be harmful.	'I read it' = ad populum; 'I don't see how' = appeal to ignorance; also, hasty generalisation to 'Playboy' (as opposed to other porn) and on arguer's own experience.
Feminists might criticise me for looking at porn, but they shouldn't talk; they obviously look at it, too, or they couldn't criticise it.	Tu quoque; equivocation on 'look at' (reading something to critique it is different from reading it regularly for pleasure).
Many important people, including the presidents, writers and entertainers who have been interviewed by the magazine and the women who pose in it, apparently agree.	Ad populum and appeal to authority.
Scientific studies so far have not proved that pornography is harmful, so it must not be harmful.	Appeal to ignorance.
Feminists should take a lesson from my parents— they don't like loud music and won't have it in their houses, but they don't go around saying it's harmful to everyone or trying to prevent others from listening to it.	Weak analogy.
Ever since feminists began attacking our popular culture, the moral foundation of our society has been weakened; the divorce rate, for example, continues to rise.	Post hoc ergo propter hoc; divorce rate = red herring.
If feminists would just cease their hysterical opposition to sex, perhaps relationships in our society would improve.	'Opposition to sex' = straw man; 'hysterical' = ad hominem.
If feminists insist, instead, on banning porn, large numbers of women will be jobless and will have to work as prostitutes to support themselves.	Slippery slope; did anyone actually suggest a ban?
In light of these consequences, feminists shouldn't be surprised if their protests are met with violence. Truly, the feminist argument is baseless.	Ad baculum: a fallacy not discussed above, in which the arguer says, 'If you don't agree with my conclusion, bad things will happen to you.' And saying the feminist argument is baseless begs the question – this is not additional evidence, but the exact claim the writer is hoping to establish (with 'baseless' in place of 'has no merit').

Source: From http://www.unc.edu/depts/wcweb/handouts/fallacyargument.htm.

REFERENCES

Browne, MN and Keeley, SM (2007) *Asking the Right Questions: A Guide to Critical Thinking*, 8th edition. Upper Saddle River, NJ: Pearson Education.

Cottrell, S (2005) *Critical Thinking Skills*. Basingstoke: Palgrave Macmillan.

Dewey, J (1933) *How We Think: A Restatement of the Relation of Reflective Thinking to the Educational Process*. Lexington, MA: DC Heath Publishing.

Ennis, RH (1964) *The Cornell Critical Thinking Tests*. Available online at http://faculty.ed.uiuc.edu/rhennis/cornellclassreas.pdf (accessed 19 October 2009).

Glaser, E (1941) *An Experiment in the Development of Critical Thinking*. New York: Teachers' College, Columbia University.

Judge, B, Jones, P and McCreery, E (2009) *Critical Thinking Skills for Education Students.* Exeter: Learning Matters.

FURTHER READING

van den Brink-Budgen, R (2000) *Critical Thinking for Students*. Oxford: How To Books.

USEFUL WEBSITES

www.criticalthinking.com (books and software to aid critical thinking for students)

www.criticalthinking.org.uk (Critical Thinking's *Criteria of Credibility*)

www.logicalfallacies.info/ (more about the logical fallacies discussed in the chapter)

www.unc.edu/depts/wcweb/handouts/fallacyargument.htm (contains the sample argument used in the chapter, plus a less fallacious argument making the same claim)

5 Collaborative learning

Introduction

The principle of collaborative learning is that people will learn more effectively when they work in a group, where they support each other, share ideas and offer constructive criticism, than they would in isolation. This is supported by research identifying the benefits of working in groups, suggesting that:

individuals who either worked in or observed groups showed significantly greater improvement in performance than did individuals who worked by themselves.

(Olivera and Straus, 2004, p455)

You can learn by observing others, working in collaboration with others on a shared goal or task and by sharing your ideas. You may have noticed that it is not until you have explained to another person an idea or process that you feel you understand the topic at a deeper level. The thought process involved when explaining an idea to a third party appears to be beneficial to your own learning process.

Collaborative learning is all about working as a team for the benefit of the individual members of that team; the expectation is that together you achieve more. This chapter will identify the benefits of collaborative learning; consider a model of group formation and change postulated by Tuckman (1965); and identify the ideal contents of meetings during the management of a project. The nature and characteristics of a group are considered and the effects of aggressive, submissive, manipulative, compliant and assertive behaviours are discussed. Further, the new concept of academic assertiveness is introduced and the work of Belbin is examined, identifying typical characteristics of group members. Finally, conflict and conflict management resolution are considered, along with a number of suitable coping strategies.

PRACTICAL TASK

Before reading on, consider and list what the benefits may be of working with others collaboratively. Write your answers below.

....

....

....

....

....

....

The benefits of collaborative learning

Some of the benefits of collaborative learning are that you:

- identify and share a common goal;

- respond to other people's questions;

- consider a topic from other points of view;

- share in the process of communal learning;

- share a common dependency.

The reasons for the success of collaborative learning are that, by working with others, you benefit from their interpretations of a topic. Even if another member of the team misunderstands some aspects of a given topic, idea or argument, this can still benefit you as you are able to explain to them your own understanding. It is no accident that people learn in groups; this occurs because it is an effective means of learning when ideas are shared and sparked from one person to another.

Have you ever noticed how painful the process of computer-based training (CBT) can be? You sit there in front of a screen pressing the next button, time after time, in a form of robotic solitary confinement. The computer software does not take into account your own thought processes and does not allow you to ask questions as they appear in your mind. You are stuck like a tram to the rails, as the computer program guides you along someone else's understanding of the subject matter. Alternatively, when learning about a subject with other people, the interaction with others is immediate. You can discuss topics until you feel you properly understand them and there are plenty of opportunities to ask questions. It is the exposure to various perspectives that is the key here.

There are many ways to know something and, when knowledge is constructed effectively, the connections or links between discrete ideas become more obvious to us. It is not always the ability to know something that is key to understanding it; it is the ability to contextualise knowledge and make relevant links that is the crucial element of knowledge. Collaborative learning assists the process of constructing knowledge because it offers multiple perspectives. As a result, the participants benefit from each other in multiple ways.

Consider this: if a group of ten people has ten apples and each person swaps their apple(s) with another person, they still have one apple each. No matter how many times the apples are swapped, no more than ten apples exist. However, if each member of a group were to swap his or her ideas with another person, each person now has two ideas and so on. Therein lies the value of collaborative learning; it is far greater than the sum of its parts.

As you work with others and get to know the individual members better, you may notice that the group changes in nature. This is a common phenomenon and worthy of study as it will have a direct effect on your contribution to the group and subsequently your own learning.

Group development

Whenever several people work together towards a common goal, a general pattern of behaviour can be observed as the individual members of the group begin to function as part of that group. A group will need to sort itself out before it can function properly: a pecking order, roles and responsibilities will need to be addressed; this is referred to as group development. It was Tuckman who offered a model for group formation when he suggested four stages of development in his paper 'Developmental sequence in small groups', first published in 1965. Although it has been some time since the introduction of this theory, it remains influential even today, as no one has yet come up with a simple yet effective model. He suggested that, as a group forms, it would go through four stages:

- forming;
- storming;
- norming; and
- performing.

Stage 1: Forming

When people come together in a group they have a desire to be accepted by the others in the group. This overrides all other considerations; as a result they avoid disagreement, argument or conflict. At this stage any activity is centred around the organisation of the group, individual responsibilities and considerations of when and where to meet. However, under the surface a great deal is going on, which will come into play later. This includes gathering information about others, making general impressions of other group members, social networking and various judgements of others. This is a relatively peaceful stage to be in, as there is a general avoidance of conflict; no one wants to upset the apple cart – yet. This does mean that not much actually gets done beyond a quite superficial level. Within a group there are roles to be claimed, such as leader, joker, helper, expert, etc., and everything is up for grabs. However, as these are sought after, disagreement can emerge.

Stage 2: Storming

At this stage something will be triggered that will pave the way for confrontation. Often the issues will relate to the roles and responsibilities of the group and may include expectations and assumptions about other people. Not everyone will desire that confrontation, but it will occur nevertheless. The level of storming will be dependent upon the nature of the organisation and the personalities within the group. For example, within the Police Service it is unlikely that the storming will amount to much, as members of the organisation are acutely aware of the consequences of disagreement between ranks or grades within this disciplined organisation. Storming will nevertheless occur.

Stage 3: Norming

Following the outbursts within the storming stage, issues have been resolved and the various responsibilities have been established. The roles that were on offer have been allocated. Expectations have been discussed and there are now fewer assumptions. Some views will have changed and the individuals are better able to understand each other's points of view. The transition experienced previously may not have been totally pleasant and, as a result, the participants may be reluctant to return to the storming stage. The individuals are now working as a cohesive group.

Stage 4: Performing

At this stage the group is in a position to perform effectively. There is an element of trust and interdependence. As there is no confrontation within the group, the participants are able to concentrate on the task in hand. There is flexibility in relation to responsibilities, and roles will be exchanged in relation to the various performance needs. This will remain until a new person joins the group, when the process may start all over again.

Tuckman refined and developed the above model in conjunction with Jensen in 1977 with the addition of a fifth stage: mourning.

Stage 5: Mourning

This is a stage that will be experienced when the group comes to an end. Generally people find endings a difficult experience, and as a result there is a tendency to not want to let go. Often the members of the group will be exchanging emails and telephone numbers with requests to stay in touch. There is a keen sense of loss felt by the group.

It is useful to be aware of this process if you are either working in a team or if you are a team leader. You will recognise that there will be fractious behaviour between members of the group, but rather than preventing this behaviour it may be best to ignore it. On occasion the team leader will instigate a discussion or argument in the knowledge that raising the issues will clear the air and enable the team to perform.

PRACTICAL TASK

Think about a time when you left a group of people or a group came to a natural end. How did it make you feel? What was said and done by the group members in response to these feelings? Write your answers below.

....

....

....

....

....

....

The prerequisites for a capable learning team

The number of people within a learning team is an important consideration. Four to six people is considered an ideal number. Fewer and there is no group dynamic, more and the group begins to split into various subfactions. Further, with a larger team it is difficult to ensure that everyone is fully involved.

You have a choice: you can promote autonomy by allowing the group to self-assign membership; alternatively, the tutor can assign membership. In general, the group will benefit from being selected as this ensures a greater balance of skills and experiences. The value of a group is the total sum of the experiences and diversity of backgrounds within it and, although like tends to attract like, this may not be best for the group. Considerations should be made to create a mix of the six strands of diversity, for example by ensuring a combination of:

- race;
- religion;
- gender;
- sexual orientation;
- age;
- disability.

The start of any experience is important and the group will benefit from understanding issues of group development. Ground rules can be negotiated, normally by the tutor or nominated leader, who will facilitate a discussion. This person's role is to provide alternatives and not to offer solutions, especially where members of the team are not working together very well, as this will interfere with the group development.

Some of the ground rules you can include are:

- acceptable levels of behaviour, including language;
- the need to attend on time;
- the importance of discussions focusing on issues and not personalities;
- issues of confidentiality;
- the responsibility of each group member to contribute to the group;
- the responsibility of the group members to value each other's contributions;
- the ability of the majority of the group to expel an individual who is not cooperating, where all attempts at inclusion have been tried and have failed;
- the right of an individual to leave a group at any time;
- a commitment to pursuing a group goal;
- the right to make mistakes and ask for help.

The content of the meetings during project management

The meetings will benefit from structure. Table 5.1 offers suggestions for inclusion and, below it, is an explanation of the contents of the table.

Table 5.1 A proposed structure for meetings

What	How
1. Introductions	Informal presentations including previous experiences, interests, qualifications and perceived abilities.
2. Roles and responsibilities	Allocation of group leader, minute keeper and other roles as necessary.
3. Ground rules	Discussion by group.
4. Purpose of meetings	To establish what the group wishes to gain from the meetings.
5. General procedures	Discussion in relation to the procedure to be adopted, length of meetings, etc.
6. Communication channels	Email contact list, phone numbers, etc.
7. Identification of learning outcomes	Identify the objectives of the group.
8. Planning	Identify objectives, timeline and milestones, Gantt chart and completion date.
9. Allocation of tasks	Allocate individual tasks, e.g. internet research, library research, environmental scanning.
10. Product	Identify the end product; will it be a presentation, assignment or e-portfolio?
11. Project development	Identify progress, consider milestones and risk assessment.
12. Mid-term review	Identify the progress to date; what has been achieved, what needs to be achieved?
13. Product	Identify completed product.
14. Analysis	Review the achievement of the group.
15. Closure	Identify the end of the project.
16. Evaluation	Review the effectiveness of the procedure before embarking on the next project.

Explanation

1. **Introductions**: Each member of the group shares with the other members the qualities that they believe they can bring to the group, listing their strengths and weaknesses. This will enable the group to identify a suitable role for each individual.

2. **Roles and responsibilities**: Having identified the perceptions of individuals in 1 above, roles are allocated on the basis of suitability, need and a willingness to cooperate. If an individual is unhappy about the allocation of a particular role, it may be possible to rotate responsibilities to ensure equity.

3. **Ground rules**: Issues of behaviour and protocol are considered at this stage. It is useful to record these accurately and perhaps on a flip chart, as often they are referred to during subsequent discussions during Tuckman's storming stage.

4. **Purpose of meetings**: This is all about managing expectations. Often people assume that certain things will happen and, if these expectations are not met, allegations of

breach of contact may occur. In fact, if no contract is discussed then no breach can occur, but it is not uncommon for people to assume that their own thoughts and feelings are shared by the group. It is far better to discuss the purpose and general aim of the meeting to prevent assumptions and misunderstandings.

5. **General procedures**: This is a discussion to decide on the general procedures of the meeting, for example who should speak when, the length of meeting, what to do about non-attendance, the regularity of meetings, etc.

6. **Communication channels**: Using technology, it may be possible to communicate ideas and progress using emails, texts and phone calls. This will have the effect of reducing the frequency of the meetings, freeing up more time for research, actual work and project management.

7. **Identification of learning outcomes**: Generally, learning outcomes begin with an action verb. As the learning outcomes are usually situational, the topic chosen for this example is shoplifting by the middle classes. So ask yourself what you want to achieve and the learning outcomes could be to:

- define the term 'middle class';
- define 'shoplifting';
- state the cost of shoplifting to the UK in a 12-month period;
- identify the underlying reasons for shoplifting by the middle classes;
- explain the link between the extent of shoplifting and the health of the economy;
- describe what is meant by the term 'stealing to sustain a standard of living';
- compare the traditional professional shoplifters with the new amateur middle-class shoplifters;
- compare shoplifting to burglary and car crime.

Careful consideration of accurate learning outcomes could prevent wasting time if the group is not exactly sure of what the learning outcome actually is.

8. **Planning**: A project must have a start and finish date. A timeline will indicate the amount of time available and any milestones along the way. A Gantt chart is a more advanced timeline. It takes the form of a lateral bar chart indicating start and finish times and further identifies where one activity may be dependent upon the completion of another. The popularity of the Gantt chart has increased with the use of computers.

9. **Allocation of tasks**: Within any team, there will be strengths and weaknesses, for example some people in the group will be happy to research material in a library, while others will be better suited to researching on the internet. The choice is yours; you can either pair people up with the more able assisting the less able or, if time is short, allocate the jobs to the more able.

10. **Product**: Identify the end product. What are you striving to achieve as a team? Will you be writing a report or an essay or delivering a portfolio?

11. Project development: As the project develops, it is good practice to keep an eye on the milestones. The term 'milestone' is given to an event that should be achieved at a given time, for example the completion of desktop research. If it appears that milestones will not be met, then this could increase the risk to the project. If this is the case, more time will need to be given to the task.

12. Mid-term review: This is a more formal form of project development and is a time when roles and responsibilities can be re-examined in the light of progress. It is a suitable time to employ gap analysis. This means you identify what you have achieved, compare that to what you wanted to achieve and then identify any gaps between the two. If gaps do exist, a strategy must be considered to get the project back on track.

13. Product: At the end of the project you will need to identify when to stop. Sometimes perfection is desired by some members of the team. Knowing when to stop is a skill. Sometimes good enough is good enough.

14. Analysis: At the end of the project review the achievement of the group. How well did they function? What has been learned about individual performance? (Remember, you assess people and evaluate the project/process.)

15. Closure: When the product has been achieved, it is time to close the project. For some people, this can be difficult and is akin to Tuckman's mourning stage 5 (see page 74). It may be appropriate to mark the end of the process with a celebration of some kind.

16. Evaluation: Consider the chosen procedures, protocols, practices, etc. Did they work? How can they be improved? What can be done differently the next time?

The nature and characteristics of a group

Working with others will always be problematic; people have their good and bad days and are affected by any number of influences. Personalities can and often do clash. Tolerance of others and mutual respect are important qualities when working in groups. As a police officer, you will recognise the importance of these qualities when dealing with less easy individuals, and these skills will be very useful when working as part of a group. One underlying reason for misunderstandings between individuals when working together can be shown in the form of a bipolar axis:

Product  Process

Some members of the group will be focused on achieving the end goal – the product. Others will be more interested in how they get there – the process. Tensions can arise when one person's desire to achieve the product can interfere with another person's enjoyment of the process of actually getting there. These two positions are representative of people's values. A group will function well if the members can accept each other's values, which can only be accepted if they are identified and understood. Understanding can be achieved in an environment where people feel safe to express their views, needs and wishes.

Unconditional positive regard

Unconditional positive regard is a term introduced by the humanist, Carl Rogers, which is useful when dealing with others' values. Employing unconditional positive regard means you accept a person regardless of who they are, how they look, what they say, what they do, etc.; it is a non-judgemental approach to others. It is very difficult to achieve but worthwhile to pursue because it prevents you judging others. If you judge others, perhaps subconsciously, your attitude will exhibit itself in your behaviour as you interact with them. If this behaviour is unfavourable, this may lead to antagonism or enmity on the part of the other person, who may react unfavourably towards you in response to your behaviour. Unconditional positive regard will mean that you take responsibility for your own behaviour and ensure that you don't prejudge others or base any speculation you may have in relation to their character on unfounded assumptions. We will now consider a useful model that indicates the link between attitude and behaviour.

Batari's box

A model that you may recognise from your officer safety training is that of Batari's box:

> *This model indicates the way in which two people can upset each other within seconds without actually meaning to do so. If you are in a bad mood or you are cross about something, the chances are that it is going to affect your attitude; sometimes unconsciously. This is fine for as long as you are alone, but when you interact with someone problems can occur. This model suggests that your attitude affects your behaviour, which affects their attitude, which affects their behaviour; this is simple yet pertinent. When you meet another person, if you are carrying negative thoughts, it is possible that they will show through. In which case your attitude is at that time negative and as a consequence this will have a direct bearing upon your behaviour.*
> (Roffey-Barentsen and Malthouse, 2009, p51)

Batari's box (see Figure 5.1) is a useful model to consider when examining human interaction in groups because it highlights the need to consider your own attitude and the effects it will have upon others. Working with other people will certainly not be without its

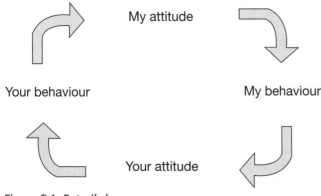

My attitude

Your behaviour

My behaviour

Your attitude

Figure 5.1 Batari's box

difficulties, but if you become aware of the effect your attitude may have on your own behaviour, it may mean that you will not upset the group.

To determine whether your behaviour is upsetting others, you will require feedback in some form. This can be at your request, or it can come about as a response to your own reflective practice, thinking about what happened and your role in that process. In which case, if you notice another person's reaction to you was unfavourable, you can think back through the conversation and ask yourself what you did, felt or said, that may have upset the other person. The trouble with behaviour is that, on some occasions, it is appropriate and on others it is not. What is required is for you to work out which is which. However, there are certain types of behaviour that can be identified as being generally inappropriate on all occasions and, as such, being detrimental to a group. For a group to function at its best, certain behaviours may be inappropriate. Four examples of inappropriate behaviours are now considered.

Aggressive and submissive behaviour

Aggressive ◄————————————► **Submissive**

Gardner (2004) describes aggressive behaviour as standing up for yourself in a way that infringes the rights of others. It is associated with an arrogant disposition, which assumes that you are right and that anyone who may contradict you is obviously wrong. The common attributes of an aggressive person include using threatening and aggressive behaviour to dominate others.

Conversely, Gardener describes a submissive person as one who does not wish to upset others, does not say what they mean and is inclined to blame themselves for things that go wrong. The common attributes of this person are those of not getting into an argument, readily accepting fault, low self-esteem and a submissive demeanour. Bishop (2006) suggests that the root of these behaviours can be traced back to early childhood where, on the one hand, a smiling and well-behaved child was rewarded with a return of smiles, compliments and attention. On the other hand, a child that was receiving no attention would gain this by misbehaving, in the knowledge that any attention, even in the form of chastisement, was better than none.

Both the aggressive and submissive positions are easy to recognise because they are things that people actually do. What is less easy to observe is manipulative and compliant behaviour.

Manipulative and compliant behaviour

Manipulative ◄————————————► **Compliant**

Manipulative behaviour is similar in effect to aggressive behaviour, but differs in that it relies more on the cognitive process than an observable behaviour. In other words, it is much to do with a person's attitude, which is not necessarily displayed to others. A person who exhibits manipulative behaviour relies on cunning and deceit. As with aggressive behaviour, there can be evidence of bullying but at a much more subtle level. An example of manipulation could be doing very little work on an assignment in the knowledge that, right at the last minute, a friend or relative will assist by giving up their valuable and busy time as an act of kindness practically to write the assignment for you. In reality, this was calculated to happen well in advance. Another example could be where you are on duty and an emergency call comes up for you to deal with just before the shift is about to finish. You claim to a colleague that you have a very important engagement that can't be cancelled, in the knowledge that the other person will volunteer to attend the call. In fact, there never was a prior engagement.

Compliant behaviour is often seen as a reaction to manipulative or bullying conduct. People exhibiting this behaviour will be keen to maintain the status quo; they may be inclined to worry about others' well-being and, as a consequence, put themselves last so that others can be kept contented. For example, at the police station, on parade, a volunteer may be requested to work a 4 p.m. to midnight town centre patrol on a Saturday night and the request is met with silence. The compliant person may feel obliged to volunteer in the knowledge that no one else had put up their hand and, in any case, the job had to be done and the others had young families. In reality, the others kept quiet because they knew you would volunteer and they were going out, but not with their families.

Neither bullying nor submissive, manipulative or compliant behaviour is conducive to group cohesion, as problems of equity arise and, as a result, feelings of animosity and injustice may be experienced. People often behave in one of these four ways because such behaviour was learned in childhood and it worked for them at that time. However, in adult life it may work, but it is inappropriate. In order for a group to function well, another more appropriate behaviour is necessary – assertiveness.

Assertive behaviour

Between aggressive–submissive and manipulative–compliant behaviours is assertive behaviour (see Figure 5.2).

Assertiveness is described by some as the ability to say 'no' to another, but there is more to it than that. It is described more accurately by Hinton, who suggests that:

Being assertive means respecting yourself and other people; seeing people as equal to you, not better than you or less important than you. The goal of assertive behaviour is to stand up for your rights in such a way that you do not violate another person's rights. It is achieved through open, direct and honest communication, valuing others, listening, respecting, problem solving and negotiating with other people.

(2009, p1)

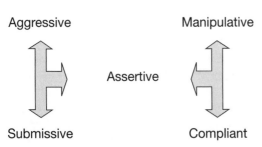

Figure 5.2 Assertive behaviour

Back and Back (2005, p1) offer two definitions of assertive behaviour:

> *Standing up for your rights in such a way that you do not violate another person's rights.*

> *Expressing your needs, wants, opinions, feelings and beliefs in direct, honest and appropriate ways.*

Assertiveness can appear to be similar to being aggressive, the notable difference being that assertive people can express themselves in a way that respects the other person. Aggressive or manipulative people do not consider the other person's point of view; they will take at the expense of others.

PRACTICAL TASK

Consider the following statements and identify them as being aggressive, assertive or submissive.

Person 1: 'You are late; you're always late. Why can't you make the effort to get in on time? You are totally useless.'

Response from Person 2: 'I admit I am late today; please accept my apologies. However, I take issue with you on the fact that you consider that I am always late. I have childcare issues and we have spoken about these in the past. If you would like to discuss this further I would be pleased to see you at your convenience.

Person 1:   Aggressive   Assertive   Submissive

Person 2:   Aggressive   Assertive   Submissive

Person 3: 'I hope you don't mind me bothering you like this, but you see the thing is that the others have said you are getting in late. I have no issue myself, but they seem to think it is unfair and we wouldn't want to upset the others, would we? Maybe you could, perhaps you know, make a little more effort. I don't mean to be rude and I quite understand how you may feel. I'm sorry for taking so much of your time.'

Person 3:   Aggressive   Assertive   Submissive

Person 4: 'I have noticed you have been late on four occasions this month. I recognise you have childcare issues. Has the situation changed since we spoke last? Is there something we should discuss?'

Person 4:   Aggressive   Assertive   Submissive

Person 5: 'It's not fair, I'm not the only one who is late. What about the others, why aren't you speaking to them? This is victimisation; if you carry on like this I'm going sick with stress. We'll see what the Federation thinks about this!'

Person 5:   Aggressive   Assertive   Submissive

(The answers are given at the end of the chapter.)

There are times when aggressive behaviour may be appropriate, for example with the use of a pre-emptive strike where you have an honestly held belief that you are about to be assaulted. However, for everyday interactions with others who are reasonable, there is no place for such behaviour. For a group to function well, assertive behaviour must be displayed by all parties.

Moon takes the idea of assertiveness a step further by introducing what she terms 'academic assertiveness', which she defines as 'a set of emotional and psychological orientations and behaviours that enables a learner appropriately to manage the challenges to the self in the course of learning and her experiences in formal education' (2009, p8). You will notice the inclusion of the word 'challenges'; learning is a challenging activity and learning in groups more so. To contextualise the above definition, Moon offers a number of examples.

PRACTICAL TASK

Consider the examples below. Which ones do you exhibit? Place a tick next to those that apply to you.

Example	Tick
The finding of an appropriate 'voice' or form of expression through which to engage in critical thinking or debate	
The willingness to challenge, to disagree and to seek or accept a challenge	
The ability to cope with the reality or the likelihood of not being 'right' sometimes, making an error or failing; effective recovery from these situations	
The willingness to change one's mind if necessary; the openness to feedback on one's performance (academic or otherwise)	
The willingness to listen and take account of the viewpoint of others; awareness that others can make mistakes and reasonable tolerance of their failings	
Autonomy – a willingness to be proactive; to make and justify independent judgements and to act on them	

Source: Moon (2009, p9)

Moon further suggests that the above attributes can be found in successful group work. Conducting yourself appropriately when embarking upon collaborative work will do much to influence the success or failure of a group. The way in which a person conducts themselves within a group will be influenced by the role they have, or believe they have, within that group. We will now consider the roles within a group.

Roles within a group

Within a group, certain roles can exist. It is during Tuckman's storming stage (see page 73) that many roles are up for grabs. Recognising the existence of these roles will enable you to:

- select an appropriate role for yourself;
- consider your own position in relation to others within a group;
- understand why a person appears to be in competition with you, as they make a claim to your role;
- identify the strengths and weaknesses of each role;
- be more aware of the dynamics displayed within the group.

Belbin (1993, p22) considered this topic and identified nine roles that commonly exist within a team (see Table 5.2).

Table 5.2 Belbin's team roles

Team role	Strengths	Allowable weakness
Plant	Creative, imaginative, unorthodox. Solves difficult problems.	Ignores details. Too preoccupied to communicate effectively.
Resource investigator	Extrovert, enthusiastic, communicative. Explores opportunities. Develops contacts.	Overoptimistic. Loses interest once initial enthusiasm has passed.
Co-ordinator	Mature, confident, a good chairperson. Clarifies goals, promotes decision-making, delegates well.	Can be seen as manipulative. Delegates personal work.
Shaper	Challenging, dynamic, thrives on pressure. Has the drive and courage to overcome obstacles.	Can provoke others. Hurts people's feelings.
Monitor evaluator	Sober, strategic, discerning. Sees all options. Judges accurately.	Lacks drive and ability to inspire others. Overtly critical.
Team worker	Cooperative, mild, perceptive, diplomatic. Listens, builds, averts friction, calms the waters.	Indecisive in crunch situations. Can be easily influenced.
Implementer	Disciplined, reliable, conservative, efficient. Turns ideas into practical actions.	Somewhat inflexible. Slow to respond to new possibilities.
Completer	Painstaking, conscientious, anxious. Searches out errors and omissions. Delivers on time.	Inclined to worry unduly. Can be a nitpicker.
Specialist	Single-minded, self-starting, dedicated. Provides knowledge and skills in rare supply.	Contributes on only a narrow front. Dwells on technicalities. Overlooks the 'big' picture.

Source: Belbin (1993, p22).

What do the roles tell us about collaborative learning? The list enables you not only to recognise the attributes of others, but also to recognise those of yourself and, by so doing, you will get to know yourself a little better. In turn, having found your place alongside your peers will enable you to contribute more effectively towards the group aim or goal.

Some of the characters identified by Belbin display behaviours that others in a group may find irksome or just unbearable, which may even lead to conflict. We will now consider issues of conflict and collaborative conflict resolution.

Conflict

Very often tensions appear within a group, the reasons for which can be many and varied. But often, conflict can stem from the fact that people see things from different perspectives and have different experiences of similar things. Problems occur when people believe they are right and others are wrong, and are willing to assert this strongly.

REFLECTIVE TASK

Consider the shape below (from McConnon and McConnon, 2008, p22). Is the small circle in the top right-hand corner of the front panel or the centre of the rear panel? Look again; perhaps the circle is in the centre of the front panel or even the top right-hand side of the rear panel.

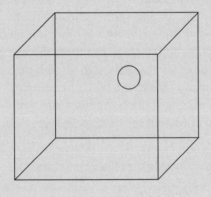

The answer to the above task is a matter of perspective and there is no right or wrong answer. If you try hard you can make yourself view the circle from other perspectives and sometimes your brain will do it for you subconsciously. If there are four possible perspectives of something as simple as a box and a small circle, imagine the perspectives of something more complicated, such as the interpretation of the law. There is a whole world out there to be interpreted differently by different people and that is just what happens.

But what about different experiences of similar things? The following account from the Persian poet and philosopher, Jalal ad-Din Muhammad Rumi (1207–1273), serves to illustrate the effect of a limited view (McConnon and McConnon, 2008).

The elephant was in a dark house; some Hindus had brought it for exhibition. In order to see it, many people were going, every one, into that darkness. As seeing it with the eye was impossible, [each one] was feeling it in the dark with the palm of his hand. The hand of one fell on its trunk; he said: 'This creature is like a water-pipe.' The hand of another touched its ear: to him it appeared to be like a fan. Since another handled its leg, he said: 'I found the elephant's shape to be like a pillar.' Another laid his hand on its back; he said: 'Truly, this elephant was like a throne.' Similarly, whenever anyone heard [a description of the elephant] he understood [it only in respect of] the part that he had touched . . . If there had been a candle in each one's hand, the difference would have gone out of their words.

(Jalal ad-Din Muhammad Rumi, 2009)

There are a number of possible lessons to be learned from the above story. One is that, although you may be positive you are correct, that doesn't make you right. A limited experience of a topic or issue enables you to understand what you are dealing with in part, but you don't know what you don't know. This is synonymous with investigating a crime – you don't rely on the first account you are given to make up your mind what may have occurred; thorough crime investigation takes time, patience and a willingness to appreciate that the truth may be perceived differently by different people. Perhaps your best policy is to listen to others' points of view before asserting your own.

Collaborative conflict resolution

Group maintenance is an essential aspect of working collaboratively. Where issues arise, dealing with them quickly will prevent further damage to the group, as disagreements prevent progress (Landsberger, 2009). Where a group is not functioning well because of a disagreement, it is appropriate to resolve any conflict. This can be done either within the group or by the introduction of another person to act as facilitator. You will notice that, at this stage, following Tuckman's model, the group has resumed the 'storming' stage (see page 73). Where conflict emerges, often the most successful group is the one whose members listen to each other without the need for individuals to insist that they alone are correct.

The process of resolution may include the following activities.

1. Collate all the relevant information.

2. From the above, identify the issue(s).

3. State your position, including how the situation has affected you.

4. Listen to others' opinions.

5. View the situation from others' perspectives, not just those in disagreement.

6. Find any common ground or areas upon which agreement can be achieved.

7. Ascertain ways to resolve the issue.

8. Draw up a formal agreement.

9. Identify the procedure if further disagreement occurs.

10. Monitor the progress and reward success if appropriate.

The process of collaborative conflict resolution can be looked upon as a learning opportunity. As a police officer or a certain member of police staff, you will be familiar with dealing with conflict between other people. Within the group, you may find that you are actually a part of the problem. According to Landsberger:

Education is an excellent setting to learn problem solving and conflict resolution strategies. Whether the conflict is a classroom real-life simulation exercise or an on-going emotional experience, learning ways to resolve issues and collaboratively work through responses and solutions will teach you skills that can be applied in other settings. It can help you:

- *accept differences;*

- *recognise mutual interests;*

- *improve persuasion skills;*

- *improve listening skills to break the reactive cycle or routine;*

- *learn to disagree without animosity;*

- *build confidence in recognizing win-win solutions;*

- *recognise/admit to/process anger and other emotions;*

- *solve problems.*

(2009, p1)

C H A P T E R   S U M M A R Y

In this chapter we have explored collaborative learning and its benefits. We have also examined group formation and change and the nature, characteristics and behaviours of groups. The work of Belbin and the typical characteristics of group members were discussed and the chapter ended with an explanation of conflict and conflict management resolution.

Answers to tasks

Aggressive, assertive, submissive (page 82)

Person 1: Aggressive

Person 2: Assertive

Person 3: Submissive

Person 4: Assertive

Person 5: Aggressive

REFERENCES

Back, K and Back, K (2005) *Assertiveness at Work*, 3rd edition. Maidenhead: McGraw-Hill.

Belbin, MR (1993) *Team Roles at Work*. Oxford: Butterworth-Heinemann.

Bishop, S (2006) *Develop your Assertiveness*, 2nd edition. London: Kogan Page.

Gardner, H (2004) *Changing Minds: The Art and Science of Changing Our Own and Other People's Minds.* Boston, MA: Harvard Business School.

Hinton, A (2009) *Effective Communication and Assertiveness. A Guide for Students*. Available online at http://cs3.brookes.ac.uk/student/services/health/assertiveness.html (accessed 22 November 2009).

Jalal ad-Din Muhammad Rumi (2009) *The Blind Men and the Elephant in Islamic Thought*. Available online at www.kheper.net/topics/blind_men_and_elephant/Sufi.html (accessed 22 November 2009).

Landsberger, J (2009). *Study Guides and Strategies.* Available online at www.studygs.net/enews/index.htm (accessed 22 November 2009).

McConnon, S and McConnon, M (2008) *Conflict Management in the Workplace: How to Manage Disagreements and Develop Trust and Understanding*, 3rd edition. Oxford: How To Books.

Moon, J (2009) *Making Groups Work: Improving Group Work Through the Principles of Academic Assertiveness in Higher Education and Professional Development*. Bristol: ESCalate.

Olivera, F and Straus, SG (2004) Group-to-individual transfer of learning: cognitive and social factors. *Small Group Research*, 35: 440. Available online at Sage Journals, http://wf2dnvr6.webfeat.org/ (accessed 22 November 2009).

Roffey-Barentsen, J and Malthouse, R (2009) *Reflective Practice in the Lifelong Learning Sector.* Exeter: Learning Matters.

Tuckman, BW (1965) Developmental sequence in small groups. *Psychological Bulletin*, 63: 384–99. Also reprinted in *Group Facilitation: A Research and Applications Journal*, 3 (Spring 2001). Available online at http://dennislearningcenter.osu.edu/references/group%20dev%20article.doc (accessed 22 November 2009).

Tuckman, BW and Jensen, MAC (1977) Stages of small group development revisited. *Group and Organizational Studies*, 2: 419–27.

6 The use of information and communication technology

Introduction

This chapter considers the use of computers for the purposes of study. They are the last significant resource to be introduced to the learning forum. Arguably, they will impact upon learning as significantly as the introduction of the printed word. They are the window to the world; the conduit of more knowledge than you could ever hope to learn. The capacity of computers is vast; to use them as tools requires that you get to know their functions well. Most people get by with relatively little knowledge and, often, unless they are shown a function or shortcut, they do not improve their computer literacy.

At first, the potential of the computer was not fully recognised. In 1977, Ken Olson, President of the Digital Equipment Corporation, proclaimed: 'There is no reason for any individual to have a computer in their home' (Darlington, 2009, p1). The computer has undergone vast improvements except in one respect.

Have you ever wondered why the QWERTY keyboard is designed in the way it is? The reason is that, in 1872, James Densmore organised the typewriter hammers in the formation with which we are all familiar, to slow down the typist and so prevent the rollers from jamming (William Dean Consultancy, 2009). Fortunately, other aspects of the computer have progressed relatively quickly; for example, by the beginning of the 1990s, a Hallmark greetings card embedded with a microchip allowing it to play 'Happy Birthday' contained more computing power than existed on the entire planet in the early 1950s (cs4fn, 2009). Today your living room, or office, will contain more computing power than was used in 1969 to enable Neil Armstrong to fly to and land on the moon (Darlington, 2009). Computers make our lives easier in many ways and today it is difficult to imagine how we ever did without them. It is estimated that computers are being sold at the rate of more than four a second, which is around 400,000 a day, or 140 million a year (Darlington, 2009). The power of computers continues to double on average about every 18 months and this brings increased functionality and ease of use (Elvin, 2005). How, then, can computers assist the process of study?

Ways in which a computer can assist your study

The uses of a computer to assist study include:

- recording and organising information;
- communicating with others;
- researching and analysing data;
- looking at diagrams and videos;
- listening to experts;
- designing presentations such as PowerPoints;
- playing DVDs, MP3 files and CDs;
- conducting literature searches.

The list could go on, as the computer can assist in practically every field of study. It is a tool and, as such, its use will require honing. Unfortunately, the computer also has its drawbacks – it can be a terrible distraction. At the push of a button you can take yourself away from your dull Word document to any amount of interesting music on You Tube, amusing/interesting video clips, and sites containing gossip, tittle-tattle and scandal. The choice is yours.

REFLECTIVE TASK

Consider the following: from the point of view of a (conscientious) student, what are the three most useful functions of a computer?

(The answer is given at the end of the chapter.)

The use of a computer when writing study notes and assignments

As discussed in Chapter 3, you will be expected to engage in various writing tasks. Using a computer can free up your writing so that, even if you have not fully researched a topic, you can still make a start on your assignment. Essentially, there are two ways to approach the writing of an assignment: the regimented method and the organic method.

Regimented method

Using the regimented method involves carefully planning the structure of the essay; this can be done using the computer. There are four general steps.

1. **Study plan**: You identify the introduction, themes and arguments.

2. **Research the topic**: This involves reading your lesson notes where you identify the main themes, arguments and further reading. Read the books from the reading list. Search the internet.

3. **Assignment plan**: Having collated the information on the subject, an assignment plan is drawn up, identifying what goes where.

4. **Write assignment**: Next you write it out in full in the knowledge that you know exactly what to write and how it should be written. The writing is the very last activity undertaken. Here you are simply placing your, much organised, thoughts on paper. The assignment will be written just the once with only minor amendments being made.

The regimented method is suitable for people who are very organised and who can keep a relatively large amount of information in their heads. This represents a linear approach to writing.

Organic method

The organic method enables the writing to take place concurrently with the study and research. This suits learners who cannot keep a large amount of information in their heads at any one time. The assignment grows exponentially as the topics are read and researched and ideas and links are realised (see Figure 6.1). At the early stages it does not matter what is written down, because it can always be changed in light of the appearance of further information. Later, as direction is realised, the work can be deleted, amended

Figure 6.1
The organic method
of writing

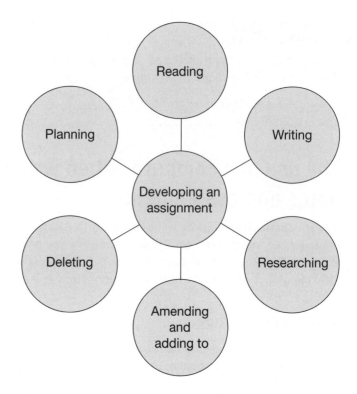

and added to. The knack is in recognising when the assignment is finished. This represents a more holistic approach to writing. Here the computer is a very valuable asset, as you are able to record, cut, copy and paste information at will. Using the computer offers you the flexibility to change things whenever you wish.

Arguably there is no right or wrong method of preparing an essay and many may be anywhere in between the regimented and organic positions. The use of the computer has freed up the writer in ways that a person who had only worked with pen and paper could not have imagined. It is recommended that a Word document is utilised for the process of writing. This will enable you to benefit from the array of tools available to assist your text. Later in the chapter you will read how to use your computer efficiently by using these tools.

Using the internet

Search engines

Whenever you do a search, on for example Google, you use what is referred to as a search engine. According to Boswell:

> *A search engine is a software program that searches for sites based on the words that you designate as search terms. Search engines look through their own databases of information in order to find what it is that you are looking for.*

> (2009, p1)

Some strange terminology is used to describe what happens, but the search engine will use what are referred to as 'spiders' or 'knowbots' to do the searching (Boswell, 2009). The most common search engines are described below.

- **Google: www.google.com** is the largest of the search engines. It uses a ranking system that promotes the use of links; the more quality links a site has, the higher it is ranked (Ó Dochartaigh, 2007).

- **Yahoo: www.yahoo.com** uses a ranking system that considers a site's popularity and relevance, but in a different way to Google. As a result, different results can be found for the same search.

- **Ask.com: www.ask.com** ranks the results to a search by 'subject-specific popularity', which means that it favours sites that are closely related in subject.

- **MSN.com: www.msm.com** ranks sites as to the relevance of the sites' contents to your search plus the number of links associated with them. Although much smaller than Google, it benefits from having some unique advanced search features.

Metasearch engines

Metasearch engines employ a number of search engines to do the searching. Metasearch engines include:

- Clusty;
- Dogpile;
- Excite;
- Metacrawler.

Specialised search tools

As their name suggests, specialised search tools are more focused search engines that are capable of capturing what is referred to as invisible web material. According to Crystal:

> The invisible web is the hidden area of the Internet that is not searched automatically by search engines. It is information that is freely available on the Internet, but that will not be retrieved by normal search requests. The information that is hidden on the invisible web takes a little more work to find . . . The invisible web is sometimes referred to as the deep web. If you think of the Internet as a giant database, some of the information on the database is easier to find than others. The information held on the visible web is just a fraction of the information available on the Internet.
>
> (2009, p1)

Examples of these search tools include:

- CNET's Download.com;
- Directory of online access journals;
- Isomics;

- Scirus;

- USA.gov.

Google Scholar

Google Scholar provides a simple way to broadly search for scholarly literature. From one place, you can search across many disciplines and sources: articles, theses, books, abstracts and court opinions, from academic publishers, professional societies, online repositories, universities and other web sites. Google Scholar helps you find relevant work across the world of scholarly research.

(Google Scholar, 2009, p1)

This database goes some way to bridging the gap between the academic journals, for which a subscription is necessary, and the free internet search. However, be warned that not all the search results will be available in their full versions; in some cases, just the abstracts are available.

Academic journals

An academic journal publishes scholarly, peer-reviewed articles written by experts. The function of a journal is to distribute knowledge, not to make money for the publishers. Scholarly documentation provides the exact source, including the author and the page number, for every important bit of outside information.

(Jerz, 2009, p1)

An academic article should end with a detailed bibliography. Often footnotes or endnotes may be present that offer a list of recommendations for further reading. The article will sometimes be long, complex and possibly difficult for a non-expert to understand right away (Jerz, 2009, p1).

Many journals are available electronically and, if you are studying with a college or university, you will be given access to these as part of your course. To do this your college will subscribe to journals covering a wide variety of academic subjects. In order to access the journals electronically you will require what is referred to as an Athens Account. This is simply a personal username and password that verify you as a student or member of staff. Having an Athens Account will mean that you can access the journal from your home computer in most cases.

What about Wikipedia?

Ó Dochartaigh observes that:

Wikipedia entries can be written by anyone and altered by anyone. Although it sounds anarchic, this process has seen the development of powerful well-written and useful articles on a wide range of academic topics.

(2007, p11)

However, he offers a caveat worthy of note: 'You would not expect to use it as a central resource for a piece of academic research, or to cite it as a reliable source' (2007, p11).

Wikipedia does have its uses; it offers a wealth of knowledge that is very useful when embarking on your research. However, be aware that opinion is not fact. For example, a search on Wikipedia under 'Law enforcement in the UK' (2 December 2009) showed a picture of a Bedfordshire police Vauxhall Astra patrol car. Next to it were the words 'The Astra is the most popular patrol car in service with British Police [citation needed]'. This begs the question, according to whom? In comparison to which other vehicles? What criteria are used to judge popularity? You will notice that the brackets do indicate that a citation is needed. To their credit, a link takes you to an explanation, which reads 'To ensure that all Wikipedia content is verifiable, anyone may question an uncited claim by inserting {{citation needed}} or a similar inline template. Exercise caution when relying upon unsourced claims' (Wikipedia, 2 December 2009).

National Police Library, Bramshill

Whether you are a police officer or police staff, you can join the National Police Library at Bramshill. Jill Mussell, the Deputy Chief Librarian, observes that officers and staff are:

> entitled to become members of the National Police Library and that [the library] catalogue is available online via the NPIA website www.npia.police.uk. This enables you to search the whole range of material available from the library and then we can supply it to you.
>
> (2009, p1)

The library website is very informative, noting that:

> In today's world, information and resources are growing at an unprecedented rate and the National Police Library can make all the difference by linking you with essential information in a timely way . . . We cover all aspects of policing – police science, criminal justice, legislation, cases, training, management and social sciences.
>
> (NPIA, 2009, p1)

According to Graham Cline (2009), one of the library assistants, the services offered by the library include:

- postal loan service for hard copy material (books, pamphlets, theses);
- e-copy and photocopy delivery of journal articles;
- enquiry answering service;
- reading lists prepared on request;
- internet access to search the library catalogue;
- monthly e-mail current awareness alerts on over 120 different subject areas.

Within the library are journals relating to the police. The list is long and includes:

- *Police Journal*;
- *British Journal of Criminology*;
- *Crime Prevention and Community Safety*;

- *Criminal Behaviour and Mental Health*;

- *Terrorism and Political Violence*;

- *Child Abuse Review*;

- *Theoretical Criminology*;

- *Crime and Delinquency*;

- *Surveillance and Society*;

- *Psychology Crime and Law*.

Remember, though, that not all journals will be available electronically. If you are searching for information you don't have to restrict yourself to the e-journals. For example, on the National Police Library website under the heading 'Legal information – General legal sources', can be found information in relation to:

- Access Law;

- British and Irish Legal Information Institute (BAILI);

- Eagle-I Service;

- European Court of Human Rights;

- Old Bailey Online;

- UK Register of Expert Witnesses;

- HMSO Acts;

- HMSO Bills.

Suffice it to say, the library contains a wealth of information. If you require assistance with your study, contact the library staff via email at library@npia.pnn.police.uk or by telephone on 01256 602650. The staff are very friendly and approachable and nothing seems to be too much trouble for them. If you are studying a particular field of expertise, they will post relevant material to you. A full description of the library's services is given at www.npia.police.uk/en/5218.htm.

Use of the internet for academic writing

As discussed when considering Wikipedia, how can you ensure that the information you have found on the web is reliable? As Mussell (2009) points out, 'I don't think you can emphasise enough how much caution should be used in accepting everything which appears on the net as fact!' If you are writing academically, the last thing you want to do is include fiction as fact, therefore being cautious will be prudent. The problem with the internet is that no one person or group has overall editorial control and, as a result, anyone can write anything they wish. This was recognised in the 1990s when the use of the internet was fast growing in popularity. Before this time, you could rely on the information available to you, in the form of published texts, as being dependable. This was due to the academic publishers having a vested interest in producing quality work.

On the internet the maintenance of quality is not something that can be assumed – far from it. In fact, Deegan and Tanner describe the web environment as a place where 'anyone can have access to the information on the web if they have a computer . . . and a small amount of knowledge. And with little more knowledge, anyone can become a content producer' (2002, p108). As a result, to some extent, you are going to have to police your own searches by being critical.

Bradley (2002) considers the characteristics to look for when evaluating the authority of a resource – domain name, company logo, contact details, currency, awards, page design and who owns the site, and also stresses the need to check the site against other sources. The Open University (2009) suggests that asking the 'who', 'why', 'when' questions may assist your search for suitability of the what.

Who?

You may have noticed that there are any number of websites where the names of the authors are not indicated anywhere. Steer clear of these sites. Sometimes you may find the information you require from the 'About Us' page. However, if you have identified the authors, what you then want to know is what academic authority do they possess? The things you are looking out for are an association with appropriate academic organ-isations, other established organisations, police establishments or government bodies (those ending in .gov, for example). Consider the web address; if the site ends with .ac.uk or .edu it is a site of an academic institution and, as such, is likely to be very careful in relation to the information placed on the site. Identify whether the author has published in the subject about which he or she is writing.

Why?

Ask yourself what the reason is for the existence of the site. Does the site support what it suggests or is it there to advertise a product or promote a religion or course? Look at the surrounding pages; what do they contain? Is the information provided likely to be reliable? If it supports the sale of a product, its reliability will be questionable.

When?

When was this site built and when was it last updated? A well-maintained and up-to-date site can be indicative of its suitability. If you are searching on the internet, the chances are it is because you are seeking for the latest material. Steer clear of sites that have not been updated for a number of months.

Searching on the web

The problem inherent with searching on the internet is not that you cannot find something, it is the fact that so often you find too much of something. By restricting your search to ask for exactly what you want should enable you to improve the effectiveness of your search. Boolean logic is employed when searching the internet and takes its name from the mathematician, George Boole. Essentially, the logical relationships between terms can be modified by the use of three words:

- OR

- AND

- NOT.

For the sake of explanation, let's say you have been tasked with identifying a spate of emerging crimes that are suspected of being committed by the same organised gang. The modus operandi (MO) is such that links have been observed between crimes committed in London and Manchester. Consider the Venn diagram below, indicating:

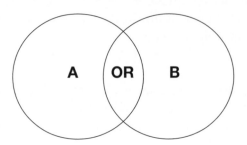

This search follows the Boolean logic by searching for the type of crime both in London **OR** Manchester. It will consider both, so your results will be a sum of the two.

London **OR** Manchester	2,360

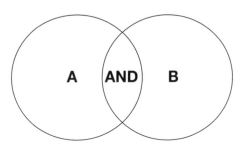

This second search follows Boolean logic by searching for the type of crime that has occurred in both London **AND** Manchester.

London **AND** Manchester	525

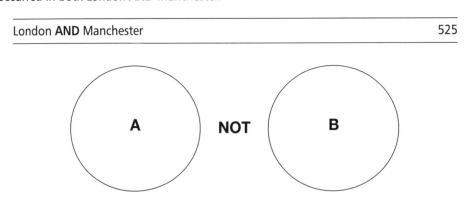

This searches for the type of crime that followed the same MO as before but only in London and **NOT** in Manchester.

A London	1,500

Leaving Manchester with the following statistic:

B Manchester	860

Being aware of Boolean logic will help you think appropriately when searching on the internet. Symbols can be used and these will be identified later in this chapter.

Advice re general search queries

Clegg (2006, p16) offers some simple rules for generating search queries and suggests the following questions and advice:

- **Do I know which website to go to?** If so, go straight there.

- **Am I looking for a simple, single piece of information?** Type it straight into a search engine, or an online encyclopedia.

- **Do I know anything about this subject?** Think up an appropriate set of keywords that will home in on your topic.

- **Break down the requirement.** Look for different parts of the brief that will produce separate searches. Watch out for keywords that are best combined in double blips to make a phrase.

- **Is it about a person?** It's worth trying the person's name with the keyword *biography*.

- **Scan the first summary results.** Look out for patterns, repeated responses and keywords that will be useful for further searching.

- **Don't worry about discarding.** If a search leads you to a dead end, don't try to make something out of it, go back and start again. Be flexible and prepared to alter your keywords.

Advanced search features

The guidance in Table 6.1 restricts itself to searching on Google, but that is not to say that many of the techniques described below are not usable with other sites. Google has been chosen here because of its popularity.

Table 6.1 Advanced search features

Phrase search, e.g. "Black Panther"	Placing the words in double quotation marks restricts the search engine to the exact words and order. This will restrict the results, making them more manageable, but, in this case, would miss the name Donald Neilson, who was called the Black Panther.
Placing a minus sign before a word, e.g. –Donald Neilson	If you were searching for black panthers and found you were getting hits on Donald Neilson, you could exclude that name by placing a minus sign immediately before his name.
Placing a plus sign before a word, e.g. +Donald Neilson	If you were searching for the name, Black Panther, and wanted to include Donald Neilson, you could incorporate both by placing a plus sign immediately before the name.
Using the word OR, e.g. Crays OR Krays	There are occasions when you may not be able to spell a word, as in the example of the Kray twins, or, for example, you are unaware of the exact year that the Poll Tax riots took place. In both cases, using the word OR in capitals will include both spellings or both dates: Poll tax riots 1989 OR 1990.
Using the star *, e.g. Sweeney down to you*	The star, which is also known as the wildcard, is used when only a part of the title or sentence is known. For example, with a search on "Sweeney down to you*", the last word of the episode cannot be remembered. Using the star reveals 'The Sweeney, Down to You, Brother'.
Using the tilde ~	Used for synonyms, for example ~cops. This produces results including law enforcement, Washington police, Metropolitan Police homepage, etc.
	A synonym (from Greek syn 'with' and onoma 'name') is a word that has the same meaning as another word. An example of this is car and automobile, or cop, Bobby and police officer.

Efficient use of your computer

Whenever you take your hands off the keyboard and use the mouse you are wasting time. Any single occasion will amount to very little time, perhaps three or four seconds at most. But you can spend hours working on your computer and those seconds will add up. Acquainting yourself with the shortcuts will save you time and energy and make your time on the computer a more enjoyable experience. Below are listed some shortcuts; try learning them a few at a time. There are ways of remembering what they do by association, for example the combination of control and x is to cut and this can be remembered by picturing the letter x as a pair of scissors with which you may cut an article out of a magazine. Others are more easily remembered when the letter is the first letter of the associated word, for example control + c to copy a document.

Read through the following and ask yourself how you could remember the shortcuts.

Undo	*Control + z*	*Find*	*Control + f*
Cut	*Control + x*	*Go to*	*Control + g*
Copy	*Control + c*	*Insert hyperlink*	*Control + k*
Paste	*Control + v*	*Replace*	*Control + h*
Bold	*Control + b*	*Font*	*Control + d*
New document	*Control + n*	*Open file*	*Control + o*
Underline	*Control + u*	*Italic*	*Control + i*
Save	*Control + s*	*Align text right*	*Control + r*
Print	*Control + p*	*Align text left*	*Control + l*
Highlight all	*Control + a*	*Centre text*	*Control + e*
Enlarge font size	*Control + }*	*Close document*	*Control + w*
Reduce font size	*Control + {*	*Word count*	*Alt + t then w*

(An extended list of shortcuts is provided at the back of this book, in the Appendix.)

There are other keys that are designed to make your work with the computer easier; we will now consider these and their possible uses.

Function keys

Across the top of your keyboard are the function keys, marked as F1 to F12. The purpose of these keys will differ in relation to the type of software you are using. It is worth your while becoming acquainted with the use of these, because they do provide some very useful shortcuts, which can mean less wasted time undertaking repetitive tasks. Perhaps one of the most useful is the F4 key and, of course, Shift + F7. A list of functions is described below and is designed to help you help yourself.

F1 This is the **help** button. If you press F1 while at the Windows desktop or when the Windows Explorer is open, a Windows help screen will appear.

F2 This **moves** text or graphics. To do this, highlight your text and press F2. Next place your cursor in the new location and press enter and your text will be moved.

This will also **rename** a file when working in Windows. If you highlight a folder or file and press F2, you will be able to rename it. This is just like right-clicking a file or folder and selecting rename.

F3 This inserts **autotext**. This is a way of inserting a repeated name or phrase auto-matically.

Alt + F3 enables you to create an autotext entry. To do this, highlight a word or phrase and press Alt + F3. You will be asked to name it. Type in the name for the phrase and then press F3; it should then appear.

Shift + F3 changes the case by highlighting the word you want to change and pressing shift + F3.

F4 **Repeat** the last action. This is very useful for repetitive actions.

Ctrl + F4 will close the window.

Alt + F4 closes any Windows program.

This opens the Address bar when working in Internet Explorer. This enables you to type the address of a Web page for quick access.

F5 This is the **refresh** key. Using this ensures that you have the most current version of that Web page.

Ctrl +F5 will change the document window from maximize to whatever size you usually have it; you can change it back with Ctrl + F10.

Ctrl + Shift + F5 will allow you to edit a bookmark.

F6 F6 will take you to the **next pane** and Shift + F6 takes you to the previous pane.

Ctrl + F6 will enable you to toggle through your open documents.

F7 This enables you to check your **spelling and grammar**.

Shift + F7 provides the thesaurus.

F8 This **extends a selection**. To do this, select a word and press the F8 key, and the selection will increase in size.

Shift + F8 reverses the above selection.

F9 There is little use for this in Windows but it is of more use in MS Word.

If you create forms or mail merges with fields, you'll want to learn the various F9 combinations. It updates selected fields.

F10 This activates the **menu bar**, from which you can make your selection with your arrows.

Shift F10 displays a shortcut menu in the same way as right-clicking with your mouse.

Ctrl F10 maximises the document window.

F11 When viewing Internet Explorer, the F11 key will make all visible toolbars disappear and is used when you need to view as much of the screen as you can. Press it again to return.

F12 This is the **Save As** command.

Ctrl + F12 is the **Open** command.

Of all the shortcuts, the five most useful tasks when writing are:

- delete;

- cut;

- copy;

- paste;

- undo.

These functions free you up so that you can develop sentences and paragraphs as you study; these can then be added to with ease if you identify the need to include further, important information.

Outline view

Another useful tool is that of Outline view. It is particularly useful when dealing with long documents, such as a dissertation, and if used properly can save you a great deal of time. It can be accessed via the tool bar from View then Outline. You begin by creating your headings and then allocating a number in relation to their relative importance. In this case, a chapter heading will be allocated a 1, a subject heading 2 and subheadings 3, etc. If you are searching through a document and don't want to be distracted by the minutiae, this is where Outline view comes into its own. You can view the document by considering the headings only and then, when you want to add to a particular part, the document can be opened up at the relevant part. If when you are writing a very long document you feel that you have allocated too many words to a certain aspect and as a result it may be unbalanced, then Outline view will help you to identify this.

According to Rado:

> *It makes it incredibly easy to restructure your document. Just drag and drop a heading to move not only that heading, but all its associated subheadings and body text . . . Because this doesn't involve the clipboard, it means you can move 200 pages-worth of information from the end of a 500-page document to the beginning in less than a second, as opposed to probably 15 minutes if you'd had to select it all in the normal way and then use cut and paste.*
>
> (2009, p1)

As with any application, it will take a little getting used to and the only way to do that is by jumping in at the deep end and actually trying it out. Other relatively recent innovations that can be jumped into, but with both virtual feet, are e-portfolios and virtual learning environments, which are discussed next.

E-portfolios and virtual learning environments

Both e-portfolios and virtual learning environments (VLEs) have been made possible because of the growth of computer technology. A significant difference between the two is that, in general terms, the e-portfolio is the responsibility of the student, whereas the VLE is the responsibility of the tutor or college.

E-portfolios

According to Sutherland and Powell (2007), 'An e-portfolio is a purposeful aggregation of digital items – ideas, evidence, reflections, feedback etc., which "presents" a selected audience with evidence of a person's learning and/or ability.' More simply put, an electronic portfolio, to use its full name, is a collection of electronically generated material used to evidence a person's achievements. Identifying the benefits of the e-portfolio, Shane Sutherland (2005), Development Director of Pebble Learning and a leading exponent of e-portfolios, recognises that:

> It is the safety and security of the eportfolio which makes it a place where learners reflect much more deeply than in paper-based alternatives and where they can write and share things that they could never share in any other way. This sense of safe personal space would certainly be eroded if linked to any form of data-harvesting service, even if that service were ostensibly provided for the benefit of the learner.

It is the creation of the safe learning environment that appears to be the strong point of e-learning.

E-portfolios can include:

- text;
- blog entries;
- hyperlinks;
- multimedia;
- electronic files;
- images;
- evidence of reflective practice.

There are three main types of e-portfolios, although they may be referred to using different terminology. These are:

- developmental;
- reflective;
- illustrative.

The developmental e-portfolio is evidence or verification of an individual's achievement over a period of time, much like the collection of papers in an NVQ-type portfolio. The second, the reflective e-portfolio, includes a log of reflective practice entries over a semester or course. It can detail aspects of a student's experiences as a learner and in life.

These experiences can include social, communicational, organisational, personal and economic considerations (Roffey-Barentsen and Malthouse, 2009). Lastly, an illustrative e-portfolio provides evidence of a person's achievements and is used as a vehicle to promote an individual. It is sometimes used as a means of evidencing the necessary criteria for job applications, in which case it is referred to as a career portfolio. E-portfolios can be a mix of any of the three types listed above, the mix being dependent upon the specific need. In general, e-portfolios are personal things and are looked at with the specific permission of the individual. Sutherland (2005) adds that:

> *if the learner is at the heart of the learning process they must have absolute control of what is written, stored and shared in their eportfolio. Knowing whether or not something you write will be read by a particular audience will affect the voice of the author. Learners reflect more honestly, more openly and more willingly when they know that they control their own assets (items of value stored within an eportfolio repository).*

VLEs

The VLE on the other hand is a far more open and public place. According to the Higher Education Academy:

> *the term 'virtual learning environment' (VLE) refers to the components in which learners and tutors participate in online interactions of various kinds, including online learning.*

> *Thus, a virtual learning environment is any electronic space where learning can take place or where interactions occur.*

> (2009, p1)

A VLE is also known as a course management system (CMS) or learning management system (LMS). It is a method of delivering learning materials to students via the web, and includes:

- assessment;
- student tracking;
- collaboration;
- communication tools.

The benefit to the students is that the VLE can be accessed from both the college and via the internet, and as a result students have access to learning materials 24/7. According to the Oxford University Press:

> *There are different types of VLE, which all work slightly differently but ultimately perform the same function and can deliver the same learning materials. A Higher Education institution is likely to have a license for a VLE that fits into any one of the following three categories: off-the-shelf, such as Blackboard or WebCT; open source (often free to use and adapt but support is charged for), such as Moodle or Bodington; bespoke (developed by institutions for their own individual needs).*

> (2009, p1)

The most widely used VLEs are:

- Blackboard;

- WebCT;

- Moodle;

- Bodington.

The technology supporting e-portfolios and VLEs is progressing dynamically and constantly. Some enthuse by suggesting that:

> *The new technology on the horizon that will define the boundary of the VLE and what we want of it is the development of personal learning spaces (e-portfolios) that offer even better opportunities for personalisation, differentiation and federated teaching.*
>
> (Rosie et al., 2007)

Remember, though, the VLE is just a means of supporting learning and, as such, is only as effective as the resources that support it.

PRACTICAL TASK

This chapter made reference to the care you should take when selecting websites for inclusion in your academic work. Look through this chapter and identify four unsuitable citations. Why are they unsuitable?

(The answer is given at the end of the chapter.)

C H A P T E R   S U M M A R Y

In this chapter we have identified the ways in which a computer can assist you in your studies. In doing so, we have explored the different types and uses of search engines and have described the sources of information available from Google Scholar, academic journals and Wikipedia. We have also identified the services offered by the National Police Library. The use of the internet for academic writing has also been considered and we have described some advanced search features that can be used to access information on the internet. We have shown how to use your computer efficiently to support your study skills further and have explored the benefits of Outline view. Finally, we have identified the benefits of e-portfolios and virtual learning environments (VLEs).

Answers to tasks

Uses for a computer (page 91)

Although there are many uses for a computer, generally for a student there are three main functions:

- writing study notes and assignments;

- searching on the internet;

- communicating by use of e-mails and social networking websites such as Facebook or Bebo (an acronym for 'Blog early, blog often').

Unsuitable website citations (page 106)

1. *'In 1977, Ken Olson, President of the Digital Equipment Corporation, proclaimed: "There is no reason for any individual to have a computer in their home" (Darlington, 2009, p1)'*

The address is .co uk and the site quoted is 'Roger Darlington's world'. This site is very informative and interesting but it lacks academic rigour.

2. *'Have you ever wondered why the QWERTY key board is designed in the way it is? The reason is that in 1872 James Densmore organised the typewriter hammers in the formation with which we are all familiar, to slow down the typist and so prevent the rollers from jamming (William Dean Consultancy, 2009)'*

William Dean Consultancy (2009) is apparently associated with a small business and, further, the quotation is incorrect. In fact, the rollers were the cylindrical part of typewriter over which the paper was fed; they did not jam, but the hammers did.

3. *'a Hallmark greeting card embedded with a microchip allowing it to play Happy Birthday, contained more computing power than existed on the entire planet in the early 1950s (cs4fn: 2009)'*

cs4fn state:

cs4fn was created and is written and edited by Paul Curzon and Peter McOwan of the Department of Computer Science of Queen Mary, University of London with the aim of sharing our passion about all things to do with Computer Science. We hope you will enjoy exploring cs4fn as much as we enjoy writing it.

A science magazine does not cut the mustard.

4. *'The new technology on the horizon that will define the boundary of the VLE and what we want of it is the development of personal learning spaces (e-portfolios) that offer even better opportunities for personalisation, differentiation and federated teaching (Rosie et al., 2007)'*

Rosie, A, Reynolds, C, Smith, C, Foord, D, Cervantes, D, Lando, E, Mylchreest, F, Rebbeck, G, Kelly, G, Soares, G, Keil, H, Radcliffe, I, Edmonstone, J, Florczak, K, Daye, K, Reiling, K,

Lavery, L, Jacob, M, Hoyland, N, Wynne, N, Travis, P, Trethewey, P, Nagus, R and McCullagh, C (2007) What are the benefits of using a VLE in teaching and learning? *Best Practice Models for e-learning Wiki.* Staffordshire University Wiki. Available online at http://staffordshireuniversity.pbworks.com/Benefits-of-Using-a-VLE (accessed 22 January 2009).

The above was taken from a discussion on a Wiki (a website that enables the writing and editing of interlinked web pages). Any one of the above names could have contributed to the citation.

Remember Mussell's (2009) advice: 'I don't think you can emphasise enough how much caution should be used in accepting everything which appears on the net as fact!' And that's a fact!

REFERENCES

Boswell, W (2009) *What is a Search Engine? How Do Search Engines Work?* Available online at http://websearch.about.com/od/enginesanddirectories/a/searchengine.htm (accessed 22 November 2009).

Bradley, P (2002) *The Advanced Internet Searcher's Handbook*, 2nd edition. London: Library Association Publishing.

Clegg, B (2006) *Studying Using the Web: The Student's Guide to Using the Ultimate Information Resource.* London: Routledge.

Cline, G (2009) Email conversation with assistant librarian, IT and Enquiries, National Police Library, Bramshill, 2 December.

Crystal, G (2009) *What Is the Invisible Net?* Available online at www.wisegeek.com/what-is-the-invisible-web.htm (accessed 22 November 2009).

cs4fn (2009) Computers for Fun, Queen Mary University of London. Available online at www.cs4fn.org/vlsi/hallmark.php (accessed 22 November 2009).

Darlington, R (2009) *Fascinating Facts and Figures About All Aspects of the Information Society.* Available online at www.rogerdarlington.co.uk/fff.html (accessed 22 November 2009).

Deegan, D and Tanner, S (2002) *Digital Futures: Strategies for the Information Age.* London: Library Association.

Elvin, C (2005) *Twenty Practical Uses of a Computer for the EFL Professional.* Available online at www.eflclub.com/elvin/publications/20computeruses.html (accessed 22 November 2009).

Google Scholar (2009) *About Google Scholar.* Available online at http://scholar.google.com/intl/en/scholar/about.html (accessed 22 November 2009).

Higher Education Academy (2009) *Virtual Learning Environments.* Higher Education Academy, UK Centre of Legal Education. Available online at www.ukcle.ac.uk/resources/trns/vles/one.html (accessed 22 November 2009).

Jerz, DG (2009) *Academic Journals: What Are They?* Available online at http://jerz.setonhill.edu/writing/academic/sources/journals/index.html (accessed 22 November 2009).

Mussell, J (2009) Email conversation with Deputy Chief Librarian, National Police Library, Bramshill, 9 December.

National Policing Improvement Agency (NPIA) (2009) National Police Library. Available online at www.npia.police.uk (accessed 22 November 2009).

Ó Dochartaigh, N (2007) *Internet Research Skills*. London: Sage.

Open University (2009) *Web Guide*. Available online at http://openlearn.open.ac.uk/course/view.php?id=1505 (accessed 22 November 2009).

Oxford University Press (2009) *Learn about Virtual Learning Environment/Course Management System Content*. Available online at www.oup.com/uk/orc/learnvle/ (accessed 22 November 2009).

Rado, D (2009) *How to Save Yourself Hours by Using Outline View Properly*. Available online at http://word.mvps.org/faqs/formatting/usingolview.htm (accessed 22 November 2009).

Roffey-Barentsen, J and Malthouse, R (2009) *Reflective Practice in the Lifelong Learning Sector*. Exeter: Learning Matters.

Rosie, A, Reynolds, C, Smith, C, Foord, D, Cervantes, D, Lando, E, Mylchreest, F, Rebbeck, G, Kelly, G, Soares, G, Keil, H, Radcliffe, I, Edmonstone, J, Florczak, K, Daye, K, Reiling, K, Lavery, L, Jacob, M, Hoyland, N, Wynne, N, Travis, P, Trethewey, P, Nagus, R and McCullagh, C (2007) What are the benefits of using a VLE in teaching and learning? *Best Practice Models for e-learning Wiki*. Staffordshire University Wiki. Available online at http://staffordshireuniversity.pbworks.com/Benefits-of-Using-a-VLE (accessed 22 January 2009).

Sutherland, S (2005) ePortfolios: a personal learning space, in de Freitas, S and Yapp, C (eds) *Personalisation in the 21st Century*. Stafford: Network.

Sutherland, S and Powell, A (2007) Celtis SIG mailing list discussions (July 2007) in *Learner Portfolio*, Young, Gifted and Talented. Available online at http://ygt.dcsf.gov.uk/Community/CityGATES/JourneyElement.aspx?page=LearningPortfolio (accessed 22 November 2009).

Wikipedia (2009) *Law Enforcement in the United Kingdom*. Available online at http://en.wikipedia.org/wiki/Policing_in_the_uk (accessed 2 December 2009).

William Dean Consultancy (2009) *Cursors*. Available online at www.wdc.co.uk/pdfs/cursors2005.pdf (accessed 22 November 2009).

USEFUL WEBSITES

You may find the following websites useful in improving your use of the internet:

http://openlearn.open.ac.uk/course/view.php?id=1505 (Open Learn Web Guide offers a brief guide to making use of the web)

www.bbc.co.uk/webwise/abbeg/abbeg.shtml (Absolute Beginners' Guide to Using Your Computer comes from the BBC and is aimed at complete beginners) www.bbc.co.uk/webwise/course/ (BBC Webwise course, which is designed to assist you with the use of the internet)

www.googleguide.com (Google Guide is an online, interactive tutorial)

www.open.ac.uk/safari/SAFARI (SAFARI – Skills in Accessing, Finding and Reviewing Information – is an online course provided by the Open University and aims to help you improve your information gathering skills)

7 Presentations

CHAPTER OBJECTIVES

By the end of this chapter you will be able to:

- identify the merits of giving a presentation;
- prepare and plan a presentation;
- identify the equipment needed;
- deliver an effective presentation;
- deal with feedback and reflect on your presentation skills.

LINKS TO STANDARDS

This chapter provides opportunities for links with the following Skills for Justice, National Occupational Standards (NOS) for Policing and Law Enforcement 2008.

AB1.1   Communicate effectively with people.
AE1.1   Maintain and develop your own knowledge, skills and competence.
HA1   Manage your own resources.
HA2   Manage your own resources and professional development.

Introduction

It is not uncommon for you to be expected to give a presentation as part of your course of study or to give a briefing as a police officer and the principles for both are the same. During your course of study, giving a presentation will prepare you for a number of things:

- as part of the learning process;

- as part of an assessment process;

- to prepare you to work with others;

- to prepare you for life at work.

Following a short discussion on the merits of giving a presentation, this chapter will discuss presentations in two general parts. Part 1 covers preparing for a presentation and part 2 the delivery. In the following pages we consider how you can research and plan your presentation, develop your skills, cope with your nerves and get the most out of giving presentations.

What are the merits of giving a presentation?

There are many benefits to be gained from preparing and delivering a presentation. The skills required are:

- planning skills;
- presentation skills;
- speaking skills.

There are a number of arenas in which the ability to communicate with others in a group is desirable. An important factor is developing the confidence and skill to get up and speak to people. Although some people appear better suited to giving a presentation than others, in fact anyone can develop these skills; it is just a matter of sound preparation, rehearsal, reflective practice and the willingness to receive constructive feedback and to act upon it.

Giving presentations requires a number of social, cognitive and verbal skills, some of which may not have been practised until attending college or university.

Social skills

The ability to converse with a group of people is a skill that can only be achieved with practice. In your non-working life there may be relatively few occasions when you could practise this skill. As a police officer, you will be expected to speak to groups of people on a regular basis, for example at a local neighbourhood meeting, at a sporting event and during briefings. The principles are the same no matter what the circumstance, namely you want to communicate a message to an audience. Engaging with others in this way requires skills such as leadership, management of people and time, negotiation, communication and bargaining.

Cognitive skills

Preparing for the presentation will involve researching the topic thoroughly. This will entail reading books, journals and associated articles, searching on the internet, and general environmental scanning (having a look to see who else has given a similar presentation recently). Then there is writing in such a way that the presentation follows a logical progression. Further, if it includes an argument, you must ensure that you have considered all sides of that argument and that your line of reasoning follows a logical progression.

Verbal skills

Knowing something and verbalising something are two completely different things. For some reason, it is not until you say something that often you realise that:

- you don't know what you are talking about;

- there are gaps in your knowledge;

- you have trouble pronouncing some words;

- the structure of your knowledge requires realigning to turn what you are saying into a logical argument.

Unlike a facilitated discussion, in which the participants are expected to contribute equally, a presentation involves more of a one-way delivery of information. However, that does not preclude the prompting of discussion as a result of the information presented. The defining features of a presentation are that you have a message and a group of people to receive it.

Part 1: Preparing the presentation

Preparation

There are two questions that should be answered when preparing the presentation.

- What is your message?

- What do you want to achieve?

Both of the above may be dependent upon an important factor, namely the amount of time you have been allocated. In five minutes your message must be to the point with little by way of illustration. Twenty minutes, on the other hand, will enable you to make an impact both verbally and visually. Whatever you do, ensure that you are not trying to squeeze too much information into the allocated time. Enough is enough; no one wants to hear you rushing through the material in the hope of getting to the end.

Choosing your message

If your brief is to choose a topic of your own, select a subject you know well. That way you will be comfortable delivering the subject and will be equipped to answer any subsequent questions that may arise.

What do you want to achieve?
Think about the purpose of your presentation. Do you want to:

- educate;

- inspire;

- entertain;

- persuade?

If you have been directed to deliver a specific subject, think about the possible angles offered by the subject and select an argument or topic that will enable you to create a clear message. Careful consideration at this point will ensure later success. Remember that, although you may want to approach the subject from a different angle, being too whacky is not a good idea. At the design stage remind yourself for the need to be:

- focused;

- clear;

- relevant;

- to the point.

The planning stage will take as much effort as planning for an essay, obviously depending on what you already know about the subject. The problem you have is that you may think you know about the subject but you don't know what you don't know. The last thing you want is a question from an informed student that highlights the fact that your knowledge is sadly lacking in many respects.

The audience

Think carefully about the type of audience you will be facing. What are they already likely to know about the subject? Pitch the level of knowledge too low and they will lose interest, too high and, again, they will lose interest. It's not easy to get it just right so, if you do not know the audience, attempt to get to know about them by asking the person who is organising the presentation.

Researching

Begin by using free thinking to jot down the keywords and ideas relating to your topic. Just write things down as they come into your head. Once you have a page full of ideas, consider how the keywords and topics relate to each other and the possible direction of further research. If you have been given a reading list for the topic, ensure you refer to these and follow the other sources your research guides you towards. As you make sense of the subject, the focus of your reading will become clearer as you identify the argument of your presentation. Keep records of any references and page numbers so that you can revisit them if necessary. As you prepare and research your topic, it may be useful to draw a mind map, tree map or concept map (see Chapter 2). This will enable you to identify links, causal effects and the general shape of the subject.

What do you want to achieve?

You have a choice; the format of your presentation can:

- describe a process or procedure, such as a briefing;

- show others how to do something;

- make a reasoned argument for or against an action;

- share individual or group work;

- present your research findings;

- offer general information, help or advice.

The subject matter and the reason for you being asked to undertake the presentation will guide you to the appropriate format.

Selecting the information

Having completed the research and mapping process, it is time to make a decision about the amount of information to be included within the presentation. What is going in and what will you ignore? It is not necessary to include absolutely all there is to know about a subject, but equally it is sometimes desirable for the recipients to be given some interesting supplementary points.

As a very general principle, the rule of three is offered.

1. Tell them what you are going to tell them.

2. Tell them.

3. Tell them what you have told them.

Your presentation will be a little like a tree – the presentation tree (see Figure 7.1).

The trunk includes the main points representing the argument. The larger branches are to be taken in turn and explained to support the various aspects of the main argument. The smaller branches are used sparingly; they are representative of specific examples, for instance facts and figures that support the argument.

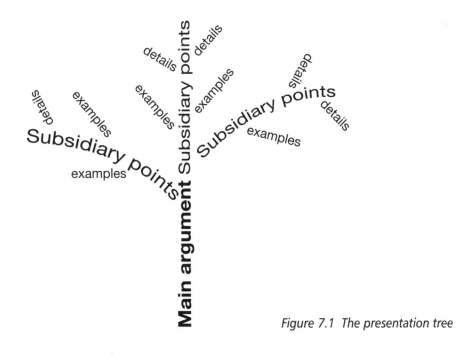

Figure 7.1 The presentation tree

Making notes

Your notes are very much like the roots of the presentation tree; they will inform (nourish) your presentation. As you write your notes, describe where on the tree you are. Signpost where you are going to assist the audience's understanding, and ensure that they recognise which branch you are on and, importantly, when you are moving from one branch (topic) to another. You need to ensure that your listeners are guided through your logical process. Summarise points before moving on, as this offers structure and assists understanding.

Structure

Clarity is important and a clear structure is a contributory feature of any presentation. Aim to have a well-defined beginning, middle and ending. If you look at the presentation tree, it has one main argument or theme and just three subsidiary/supporting branches. Remember the benefit of KISS: Keep it Short and Simple. Often, less is more.

A logical progression will assist structure. As you write your notes think about how ideas and themes marry up. For example, if the topic of your presentation was a section 10 aggravated burglary it would be appropriate to include in the presentation the definition of a section 9 burglary. So a logical progression may be to:

1. define the offence of s10;

2. define the offence of s9;

3. define 'at the time';

4. define 'has with him';

5. define 'firearm, imitation firearm';

6. define 'weapon of offence';

7. define 'explosive';

8. consider *R* v *Stones* (1989);

9. provide working examples.

Sometimes it is necessary to compare things with others so that people can identify any significant differences. Here, s9 was compared to s10 because many of the points to prove were contained within the s9 offence. Therefore, an understanding of s9 was crucial.

When considering structure, ask yourself what it is about something that makes it what it is – what are the key components? Focus on these and their relationships to the whole. For example, returning to the elephant from earlier (see page 86), it would be appropriate to describe or show the animal as a whole and then consider the various parts that make it what it is. Likewise, if you were describing a car, you would start with its colour, manufacturer and type, for example a black Aston Martin Vantage. Next, you could describe its attributes while showing a picture of the vehicle. It would be inappropriate to show the picture, discuss the vehicle and then give the name of the car, unless of course the purpose of the exercise was for the class to identify it based on your description.

You can see that there are no hard and fast rules in relation to the order in which material is designed; just ensure the order makes logical sense.

Preparing your notes

If it helps you to learn the material, write down all your notes in full initially. Later you can précis them down so they are easy to read and not a full script. As you prepare your notes, think about what it is you want to achieve, namely effective communication with the audience. Reading from a full script will not allow you to do this. Don't worry about forgetting, as sufficient rehearsal will ensure that this does not happen. Returning to the s10 example, your notes could look something like this:

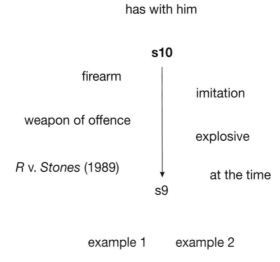

The above diagram is very brief and you would need to know your subject well. Where you rely on more comprehensive notes for facts and figures, statistics or citations, highlight these so they are easy to find. Sometimes, if your audience has lots of questions, you will not be able to finish your presentation within the allotted time. To compensate for this, identify what are called the MSCs:

- **Musts**: This material must be delivered. To ensure that it is, delivery of this material will be significantly under the allotted time.

- **Shoulds**: This material should be delivered but, if the audience is particularly vocal, it may be that some of it will not be delivered.

- **Coulds**: This is the material you keep up your sleeve so that, if your audience is very quiet and you are eating through your material, you will always have something else to rely on.

As you prepare your notes you should be considering contingency plans. You have material in the MSCs, but how do you use it? The charts below represent the musts (M), shoulds (S) and coulds (C). Your original notes have been designed for a period of 20 minutes. You will notice a number of extra Cs just in case your timing is completely out and you require more material.

M1	M2	S1	M3	S2	M4	S3	M5	S3	C2	C3	M6
								C4	C5	C6	
20 minutes										

In fact, on the day, your presentation was so interesting that the audience generated many questions. As a result you were forced to remove some of the material.

M1	M2	S1	M3	S2	M4	S3	M5	S3	C2	C3	M6
								C4	C5	C6	
20 minutes										

Your contingency plan and your MSCs enabled you to adapt your material appropriately. What do you do if you are two thirds through but suddenly realise that you have about two minutes left in which to wrap up?

M1	M2	S1	M3	S2	M4	S3	M5	S3	C2	C3	M6
18 Minutes								Go to end		

In general, presentations tend to take longer than you anticipate. You can see in the chart above that, at 18 minutes into the presentation, the speaker realised that it was time to conclude. From this point they went straight to the end to M6, which they knew would last just 2 minutes. The beauty of this is that your audience will have no idea what material they have not been given.

Designing the content

There are two places in your presentation that will be remembered, the beginning and the end; the part in the middle is less significant, so when designing the content your start and close must be strong. People like to be told where they are going, so to this end it is good practice to explain what you are going to speak about and the form it will take. Your 20-minute presentation will benefit from about three subsidiary points to support your main general argument.

Content design stage 1: Plan

Although you have researched the topic and made a mind map of the content of the presentation, it is at this stage that the design process starts in earnest. During this first stage you are simply filling in the blanks. Consider the presentation design template below.

	Tell them what you are going to tell them
Introduction	• Introduce yourself. • State main argument. • Describe what you are going to speak about.
	Tell them
Subsidiary point 1	Describe subsidiary point in detail and include supporting detail and specific examples.
Subsidiary point 2	Describe subsidiary point in detail and include supporting detail and specific examples.
Subsidiary point 3	Describe subsidiary point in detail and include supporting detail and specific examples.
	Tell them what you have just told them
Close	Restate main argument with brief supporting subsidiary points. End session.

Using the template above will mean that each stage will be considered in turn and in what you consider a logical progression. The first draft may just include the topics and a few ideas; using the computer you can gradually add to these.

Content design stage 2: Build

The next stage is to flesh the ideas out. As mentioned previously, at this stage it does not matter if you script what you wish to say as that will help you learn the material. At this stage you can consider the strategies you are going to use to engage the audience. Consider Figure 7.2, which is adapted from Petty (2004), whose observations are pertinent to presenting, although he was writing about teaching.

What can be inferred from Figure 7.2 is that, if all you do is speak to the audience, they will retain very little of what you say. The level of retained information is a consideration for you at this stage because this will influence what you do with your audience. Any of the activities listed in Figure 7.2 can be incorporated into your presentation; the choice is yours.

Content design stage 3: Practise

You will arrive at stage 3 almost without realising, because this is the time that your presentation comes together. The writing is finished and you are now in a position to practise your delivery. Remember that, even if you think you feel stupid, it is imperative that you actually speak the words out loud. This is because the part of the brain you use to think the words and the parts you use to speak the words are different and, further, you will practise speaking the sentences. It would be a disaster if the first time you were to speak the words out was during the presentation and you realised that some words were

		Ears 🔊	Eyes 👁	Voice 🔊 or Writing ✍	Doing ✎ or Touch ✋	
Listening	5%	✋				Receive information
Reading	10%		✋			
Audio-visual	20%	✋	✋			
Teacher demonstration	30%	✋	✋			
Discussion groups	50%	✋	✋	✋		Apply learning
Practise by doing	75%	✋	✋	✋	✋	
The student teaches others, or applies the learning immediately	90%	✋	✋	✋	✋	

Increasing cognitive demand →

Figure 7.2 Engaging the audience (adapted from Petty, 2004)

very difficult to present in the order in which you have written them. Timings are a consideration at this point. To ensure timings are spot on, choose moments at significant stages of your presentation. Work out the timings for these, so that, as you speak, you can see if you are in front of or behind those times. This will of course be dependent upon you being able to see the time.

Content design stage 4: Dress rehearsal
There will come a time when you will need to put yourself under a little pressure. Here a critical friend is very useful. Draw up a list of things you want that person to consider, which can include:

- body language;
- pronunciation;
- your chosen accent;
- position;
- use of non-verbal communication;
- pitch of voice;
- irritating habits;
- repeated filler words;
- the content;

- the whole package;

- unintentional consequences.

Using your notes and not the script, speak through the material and ask for constructive feedback. Don't expect all of the aspects above to be considered on every occasion, as there would be too much for one person to consider at one time. It may be better for you not to know which of the above factors are being assessed.

Content design stage 5: Reflective practice

By now you will have received feedback on your performance and you will have acted on that which you agreed with. At this stage you can begin to help yourself. The use of reflective practice will serve to inform your presentation skills. This will only occur if you are totally honest with yourself. Follow the reflective practice cycle, shown below, from Roffey-Barentsen and Malthouse (2009, p27). You can enter this cycle at any stage and, as you have been working on the presentation and receiving advice, it will be appropriate to begin from 'Action plan'. At this stage you have thought how you may deliver your presentation differently. Next, this is put into practice and, having done that, you reflect upon it, perhaps asking yourself the following questions.

- What did I want?

- What did I do?

- What is the difference between the two?

The difference will be your professional practice, in this case specifically the delivery of your presentation.

Reflective practice will enable you to make best use of one of your most valuable resources – yourself.

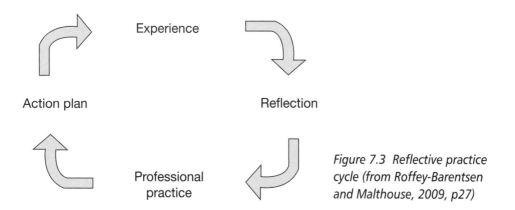

Experience

Action plan

Reflection

Professional practice

Figure 7.3 Reflective practice cycle (from Roffey-Barentsen and Malthouse, 2009, p27)

Identify the available equipment

At the earliest opportunity identify the room in which you will be delivering the presentation. Doing this will enable you to identify the equipment available to you. This could include:

- flip chart and stand;

- whiteboard;

- interactive whiteboard;

- computer;

- projector.

Flip chart and stand

This is useful if you need to express yourself visually during the presentation. You can either write on the flip chart during the presentation or ensure the material is prepared beforehand. Folding the corner is useful when turning the pages.

Whiteboard

This is used in much the same way as the flip chart; the advantage is that generally it is larger and so more material can be placed on the board. Varying the marker colour serves to highlight similarities, differences or hierarchies.

Interactive whiteboard

This is similar to a whiteboard but, as it is connected to a computer, is able to offer features such as integrated digital photographs, video clips and audio clips. Data can be moved around the screen and recorded.

Computer

A computer is a very valuable tool when designing a presentation. The Excel programme will manipulate data and produce high-quality graphic representations. Word documents are an excellent resource for the production of handouts and for recording presentation notes. PowerPoint software is designed especially with presentations in mind, enabling some very professional-looking presentations.

Projector

The projector enables whatever is on the computer screen to be shared with the audience. Make sure you identify how to switch it on and where the tools are kept to control it. Many projectors are attached to the ceiling, so it is not possible to switch them on by hand.

Preparing your visual aids

Most presentations are delivered by the use of PowerPoint. However, be warned, you can overdo it – you may be familiar with the term 'death by PowerPoint'; this is where you are subjected to slide after slide as the presenter reads from each one, normally using a very dull and nasal voice. Less is more here and the PowerPoint should be used to highlight facts, offer titles and indicate bullet points. Many advocate the use of icons or pictures within the presentation. Using cartoon characters cheapens the presentation and should be avoided.

Don't cram the slide with words. You may hear advice such as 'six lines to a slide and six to eight words to a line', or limit the number of bullet points to six or fewer. These rules are useful to a point, but should not be adhered to rigidly. The most important thing to remember is that you don't want the tail to wag the dog; in other words, the PowerPoint material is not the presentation – this is what you are actually saying, so don't let PowerPoint take over.

PowerPoint is a visual tool, therefore covering it in words may be diluting the impact as words are read and so rely on a more auditory approach. Far better to use pictures, as these can have far more impact than five bullet points. There is a place for bullet points and that is at the end of the presentation when you are recapping. Remember that the size of the font is important; the people at the back of the room have to be able to read the screen. Also, don't be fooled by the use of colour, as what looks like an impressive contrast between the background and font colour may be totally lost when projected on to a screen on a bright sunny day.

Ten tips for PowerPoint presentations

1. Select a clear font such as Arial or Helvetica.

2. Use **bold** rather than underline.

3. Beware of the special effects, e.g. spinning words or sound effects.

4. Choose your colours based on an informed view.

5. Use a font size of 20 or over.

6. Keep the presentation consistent, e.g. background and style.

7. Use pictures and icons.

8. Don't use cartoons.

9. Ensure that your software is compatible with the computer you will be using.

10. Remember that less is more.

Preparing your handouts

Your handout is representative of you; therefore, attention to detail is important. For example, nothing looks worse than a photocopy of a photocopy, which is now quite grey or so black that parts of it are impossible to read. Further, the document's borders probably no longer line up with the edge of the paper. Also don't let paper lie at the bottom of your bag so that it is now crumpled or dog-eared. Consider the layout – like a PowerPoint presentation, the choice and size of your font is important, so size 12 or 14 Arial is recommended. The style of the handout is dependent upon its use and it can take the form of:

- instructions;

- a worksheet;

- further information;

- reiteration of a presentation;

- a combination of the above.

Clarity is important, so where the handout reiterates the presentation, it should complement the PowerPoint presentation or the content of what you deliver. To this end, short sharp sentences are ideal. Where possible, a list of ideas should be bullet pointed as this is easier to read. Considering the purpose of the handout during the design process will inform the layout and content.

Part 2: Delivering the presentation

Double-checking

You previously identified which room was being used for your presentation and considered the resources available to you in the planning stage. Don't assume that they will be there on the day. Go to the room and double-check. Finding that the IT department has removed the computer for maintenance can have a major impact on your PowerPoint presentation. Leave nothing to chance. Turn the projector on and sit in various seats, asking yourself if everyone in the room will have a clear and unobstructed view of the screen. If they will not, you may be able to do something about it at this stage.

Coping with your own reactions

Before considering the presentation, it is worth taking into account the one general overriding response experienced by many – nerves. Giving presentations can be a nerve-racking experience for many people, regardless of whether the audience is known to them or not. The nerves you feel occur as a result of your body gearing itself up to do one of two primitive actions – defending yourself or running away, which is known as the fight/flight response. What is happening to you is that your body is releasing chemicals such as adrenaline and cortisol. The combination of these and other chemicals produces a number of effects.

- Your breathing quickens.

- Blood is redirected from the digestive system and pumped into your limbs.

- Your pupils dilate.

- Your general awareness intensifies.

- Your perception of pain diminishes.

- The way in which you see your environment changes.

- You feel nauseous.

- You experience what is commonly referred to as 'butterflies'.

Associated with this is a change in your mental perception, to a greater or lesser degree, where there is a tendency to view others as a threat. The fight/flight response will just kick in and you have no say in the matter at all, so there is little you can do about it. As the saying goes: there is nothing wrong with butterflies; you just have to get them to fly in formation. In other words, you know you are going to react to the situation, just ensure that you use your nerves to heighten your skills. Reducing the depth of your nervous reaction can be achieved with confidence and confidence is achieved by adequate preparation.

First impressions

It is a bit of a cliché, but valid all the same, that you only have one chance to make a first impression. How long it takes people to make that impression is a matter of conjecture. The impression you will make on your audience will be based on part fact, part previous experience and mostly assumption.

If you want to create a safe environment, first be comfortable in yourself, and this will enable others to share in that comfort. Being, or appearing to be, a rebel is not going to help. You can help yourself by conforming to those unwritten rules that you know exist. Remember, 5CS – are you:

- considerate?
- clean?
- civil?
- cheerful?
- courteous?
- smart?

If you want people to give up their time for you, listen to you and take an interest in what you have to say, the very least you can do is make an effort for them. Show some respect, which in this context means treating people as you would wish to be treated yourself. That may help your first impression to be favourable.

Achieving rapport

You have prepared, designed, practised and reflected and now is the day of your presentation. Because you are fully conversant with the material, you can now begin to think about other matters, such as how you are going to interact with the audience. This is where your own style and personality will play a part. Generally people assume a role, or character, for example:

- cheeky chappy;
- comedian;
- wise academic;

- nice but dim;

- everyone's best friend;

- military type.

The list goes on. Whether people hide behind the masks of the characters they assume or they actually are the characters they assume is a matter for debate. Those who appear to achieve rapport with the group are those who are honest with themselves and the group and are just being themselves. Rapport is not something you can demand; it just happens. It refers to a relationship between the presenter and the audience that is in balance. It occurs when there is an acceptance of roles, where the presenter is accepted by the group. Sometimes it appears within seconds and sometimes it does not appear at all.

Starting on time

A dilemma can occur when it is obvious that half the seats are empty and you are due to start. The problem is that, if you choose to wait for the latecomers, those who have made an effort to be there on time may feel undervalued. If, though, you are informed that there is a very good reason why people are not there and they will be arriving shortly, you have a choice. You can start, negotiate with those who are there on time or make the executive decision to wait. Whatever course of action you decide upon, one thing is guaranteed – you will upset someone.

Engaging with the group

At the beginning of the presentation your nerves normally disappear, which is because you have too much to think about to be nervous. You have checked the equipment and that all your resources are where you expect them to be. You move to the front of the group, stand facing them and wait for silence. You may feel sure that everyone in the room can hear your heart beating because it sounds so loud to you. Before you speak it is a good idea to negate the effects of the nerves. Unconsciously, your breathing may have been rather rapid and shallow, so take a nice deep breath as this will relax you and those around you.

Begin your presentation by introducing yourself and then introducing the topic. It is appropriate to smile but not like a Cheshire cat. Engage the audience, talk to them, look at them, speak to all of them, nod at them as you make your point and they will nod back.

There are factors that would have been considered during the design stage, and they are discussed here as they are pertinent to the actual delivery.

Language

Use a style of language appropriate to the subject matter and the audience. For example, only use jargon if you can be sure that it will be understood by all present. If you use it and feel that, by the expression of one person, it has not been understood, it is appropriate to explain its meaning in full.

Analogy and metaphor

Analogy and metaphor can be useful when explaining a concept or action. An analogy is used when identifying the similarity between two things to make a comparison, for example:

- One minute my day was quiet; the next it was just unreal. It felt like I had walked on to the film set of *Saving Private Ryan*.

- A decomposing body smells just like a very ripe camembert cheese multiplied by a thousand; it's something you don't forget in a hurry.

- To give you an idea of how I felt, it was like meeting the school bully 20 years after leaving school. You wanted to punch him hard in the face but felt it inappropriate to hit a priest.

- She had a laugh like the sound of a hyena who had been snorting helium all morning.

- I was so tired I could hardly keep my eyes open; it felt just like 4 a.m. on a night shift when your body is screaming at you to get some sleep.

- My ex-husband was much like the dog – he was untidy and smelly, came and went when he felt like it and expected me to serve him a meal whenever he walked in.

- Flying a helicopter is much like patting your head and rubbing your tummy while doing algebra with rap music turned up very loudly while having a conversation with a three-year-old.

A metaphor is a term that relates to something that is not literally applicable. It suggests a resemblance to assist understanding. It is like an analogy but is a further step removed. Here are some examples.

- He had the heart of a lion.

- It's raining cats and dogs.

- Her presentation lit a fire beneath them; their motivation rocketed.

- We must accept the cards life deals us and we alone must decide how to play the cards in order to win the game.

- On a sunny day the coastal road is a meandering river of cars.

Both analogy and metaphor will assist understanding, but try not to overdo them. Treat them as you would hundreds and thousands on a cake – a sprinkling will suffice.

The use of humour

Humour should be treated with utmost caution as others may not share your use of it. Humour should be avoided for the very reason that it is funny. This is because it pushes barriers, questions the realms of common decency, condones stereotypes, is often sexist, can make generalisations and assumptions and is often rebellious to a degree.

If you do insist on including humour, avoid starting your presentation with a joke. People will not laugh if, by doing so, there is a possibility they may alienate themselves from the other members of the audience. There is a particular expression you see on a person's face as they tell a joke and look up in anticipation of hearty laughter, only to be met with a stony silence, so try to avoid this situation. Your best policy is to avoid humour unless you know the group very well and can be absolutely sure that you will not offend any person.

Signposting

To keep your audience interested entails the need for you to make the implicit explicit. In other words, you will need to lead them through your presentation by stating what it is you are doing. Here are some examples of what is referred to as signposting.

- The main theme of my presentation is . . .
- This is supported by this, that and the other, which we will now consider in turn.
- I would like to draw your attention to . . .
- Having identified A, let's consider the implications of this. For example, how does it affect B and C?

What you are aiming to do is take the learner by the hand and explain where you are going, and what you are doing is jumping from one point to another. You cannot help this – if you have three things to describe, at some stage you must go from one to another, but failing to inform your audience of this fact may lead to confusion.

Varying the pitch and tone of your voice

Nothing is as dull as a monotonous voice reciting a presentation that has obviously been memorised and delivered on many occasions or, even worse, reading from notes. To keep your presentation alive there needs to be an element of spontaneity. This can be achieved by varying the pitch and tone of your voice in relation to the subject matter. Speeding up your delivery is another technique that will keep the audience's attention. Sometimes this is followed by a moment of silence (just for effect) and then a calmer, more measured approach follows. Experiment with this during your rehearsal to ensure that you do not come over as being a little manic.

Finishing

The end of your presentation is as important as the beginning, as these are the parts that people remember. This is due to the primacy and recency effect, which means that people remember what they heard first and last. Summarise what you have delivered and be sure to tell them that you are concluding, for example 'I would like to conclude by recapping on the main points of this presentation . . .' or 'To summarise, we saw that . . .. A cardinal sin is to say 'Just one last point . . .' three times, as the audience will very quickly become impatient with your 'one last points' because, by saying this, you have made a contract with the audience and have broken that contract.

The last sentence should tell the audience that you have finished. Some say 'And that concludes this presentation.' Others say 'Thank you for taking an interest in this presentation', or words to that effect. Be bold, smile and change your posture appropriately or move a little to one side or backwards; here you are breaking with the area you had occupied.

Reflective practice

Reflect on how you did and how you can improve your performance. Committing this to paper will enable you to capture all the salient points, which may be of use to you at a later time. Consider an action plan for the next presentation.

PRACTICAL TASK

Try creating a practice presentation on a topic that really interests you. Practise in front of a mirror to see how you will look to your audience. Record your presentation and play it back listening carefully to how it will sound. Reflect on how it looked and sounded. Identify three good things that went well and three things that didn't go well and that you need to refine and improve.

CHAPTER SUMMARY

In this chapter we first identified the merits of giving a presentation. We then went on describe how to prepare and plan a presentation, including identifying the audience and designing the content. We showed you how to identify the equipment needed and how to prepare visual aids and handouts. We then presented guidance on how to deliver an effective presentation, including the use of appropriate language and humour. Finally, we showed you how to deal with feedback and reflect on your presentation skills.

REFERENCES

Petty, G (2004) *Teaching Today*. Cheltenham: Nelson Thornes.

Roffey-Barentsen, J and Malthouse, R (2009) *Reflective Practice in the Lifelong Learning Sector*. Exeter: Learning Matters.

8 Examinations

By the end of this chapter you will be able to:

- identify the principles of memory;
- use strategies to improve memory;
- state the relationship between learning styles and memory;
- employ appropriate revision techniques;
- prepare for an examination;
- organise your revision;
- collate information about the examination;
- use appropriate exam techniques;
- adopt an appropriate writing style in your examination.

LINKS TO STANDARDS

This chapter provides opportunities for links with the following Skills for Justice, National Occupational Standards (NOS) for Policing and Law Enforcement 2008.

AB1.1 Communicate effectively with people.
AE1.1 Maintain and develop your own knowledge, skills and competence.
HA1 Manage your own resources.
HA2 Manage your own resources and professional development.

Introduction

Taking exams fills many students with dread; perhaps it is the fear of the unknown. For example, you may worry about the fact that you have no idea what will be asked and, as a consequence, no idea if you will be able to answer the question. Further, the thought that all you know about a subject should be tested by responding to a limited number of questions, using only a pen and paper and in a relatively short time, can lead many to believe that the system is unfair. This is compounded if you chose to study selectively and your chosen subjects do not come up. Exams are not generally popular but, as they are a proven method of assessment, it looks like they are here to stay. If you want to be successful in your study and exams are used, you have no option but to prepare well.

This chapter offers guidance on preparing for and taking exams. It offers advice on how to retain knowledge by identifying some principles of memory and offers strategies to improve memory. The link between your preferred style of learning and memory is explored. Revision techniques are explained and guidance is offered on how to prepare for an exam. Finding as much information as you can about the exam is recommended and suitable exam techniques are offered. Lastly, an appropriate writing style is considered for your examination. If you reflect on the advice contained within this chapter, it is hoped that your fear of exams will diminish in the knowledge that you are as prepared as you possibly can be.

Before your revision

Before you can revise, you must understand your subject fully; if you do not, no amount of revision will assist you. In fact, all you will be doing is revisiting the same half-understood material that you may either have been struggling with most of the semester or have neglected in the hope that it would just go away. The much-cited quotation from Confucius suggests:

Tell me and I will forget,
Show me and I may remember,
Include me and I will understand.

This is great, but unfortunately life is not always as simple as that – you can be included as much as you like and still not understand. There are occasions where you find the following may apply to you:

Tell me and I will forget,
Show me and I will forget,
Include me and I will forget.

There are some topics that you can find difficult to learn. For some reason, the information will not go into your head. But if you feel that you have not learned something sufficiently well, don't do nothing in the hope that the problem will simply go away – it will not. If you are aware that you will be tested on a subject, the most sensible thing to do is seek help from a tutor or peer.

Learning can be split into three broad phases.

Primary phase	**Learning**	The act of ingesting new knowledge.
Secondary phase	**Reflecting**	The act of comprehending new associations and relationships between the newly learned and existing knowledge.
Tertiary phase	**Revising**	The act of retaining that knowledge.

Revision is not part of the primary learning process and, if you treat it as if it is, you may interfere with your own learning. This is because revision is a relatively superficial process by which you remind yourself of your existing knowledge. This includes a reminder of what was learned in the primary learning phase and the relationships and links made during the secondary phase. Revision is a little like having a box of frogs with a faulty lid. Every now and again you have to collect up the frogs before they escape; the frogs represent your knowledge, which, if not visited regularly, will unfortunately be lost. So when you revise for an exam, the very last thing you want to be doing is learning in the primary phase. That process should have ended weeks or even months ago.

Memory

According to Gould, 'Memory is an information storage system and the way in which it works can be compared with another information storage system – the filing cabinet' (2009, p123). He notes the similarity of your memory system to filing a document, where a decision is made as to where exactly a document is to be stored. However, before a file can be stored it must be correctly identified and classified. This represents three processes that contribute to the sum of memory. Gould argues that, to work effectively, memory must be capable of carrying out three processes.

- **Encoding**   Information must be registered and converted to a form in which it can be stored.

- **Storing**   Information is stored and is available for future use.

- **Retrieving**   Information is recovered from storage when required.

(2009, p124)

You will notice that these two observations rely on metaphor, in this case the filing cabinet and the computer. Metaphor is useful because, when looking at the brain, the problem you encounter is that the very thing you are studying is the thing you are using to make sense of that study – you are very close to the subject. It is useful to apply a model to represent the memory process. There are many suggested models from which to select, but the Atkinson-Shiffrin model of memory is chosen due to the clarity of the process it describes (see Figure 8.1).

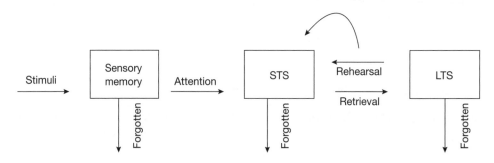

Figure 8.1 The Atkinson-Shiffrin model of memory (from Bloor and Lahiff, 2000, p23)

Sensory memory

The first box in Figure 8.1 is representative of stimuli entering the sensory memory. You are not aware of much of these stimuli due to your brain filtering the unnecessary information that would otherwise distract you. If you were to be consciously aware of all that is around you, you would not be able to function due to information overload. This information in the sensory memory lasts a very short time, unless it is acted upon, when it is forwarded to the short-term store (STS).

Short-term store

In the STS the information is made obvious to you and from this point you can choose to memorise it, otherwise it is forgotten. (It is acknowledged by the authors that this is an over-simplistic representation, as some memory will be retained without a conscious effort.) This conscious effort to remember the information can take the form of dealing with a person's name. Often, the reason why we do not remember names is because we never learned them in the first place. Repetition and association will assist memory.

Long-term store

If you have repeated the name over and over, associating it with the event and location, the knowledge may be placed within the long-term store (LTS). Sometimes this process is effortless, but on other occasions it can be a very time-consuming, tiring and taxing process.

Strategies for memorisation

Mnemonics

Mnemonics are anything used for assisting the memory. There is a variety of mnemonic techniques available to you, such as acronyms, acrostics and methods of loci.

Acronyms

An acronym is a pronounceable word made up of a series of initial letters or parts of words. Each letter is a cue to the thing you wish to remember, for example:

- **ASBO** anti-social behaviour order;
- **NATO** North Atlantic Treaty Organization;
- **Laser** light amplification by stimulated emission of radiation.

Acronyms are used extensively in police training. For example, the directions in relation to the Police and Criminal Evidence Act (PACE) have been turned into a mnemonic, GO WISELY, to help officers remember the procedure and their legal obligations:

- Grounds for search;
- Object/purpose of search;

- Warrant card (if in plain clothes);

- Identity of officer;

- Station to which attached;

- Entitlement to copy of search record;

- Legal power used;

- You are detained for the purposes of a search.

What can you do to assist your memory? Bloor and Lahiff note an important distinction between learning and remembering: 'there can be no learning without remembering: but learning and remembering are not equivalents, they are different aspects of the same phenomenon' (2000, p13). In other words, if you learn with visual stimuli, it will not necessarily follow that the information will be remembered in a visual form. There are some shortcuts to memorising that are more effective than, for example, writing something out a hundred times. The following techniques are offered for your consideration.

Acrostics

An acrostic is a useful tool to use when memorising things and is another example of a mnemonic. It is an arrangement of words in which, normally, the first letters in each line, when taken in order, spell out a word. It is the first letter of each word that is a cue to an idea you need to remember, for example:

- Every

- Good

- Boy

- Deserves

- Football.

The above is an acrostic for remembering a sequence of musical notes in the G-clef: E, G, B, D, F.

Another example could be:

- My

- Very

- Elderly

- Mother

- Just

- Sits

- Under

- Newport

- Pagnell.

Here, each first letter is representative of a planet in our solar system: Mercury, Venus, Earth, Mars, Jupiter, Saturn, Uranus, Neptune and Pluto.

The method of loci

This form of mnemonic is suitable for lists of up to about 20 things. Place yourself in a location with which you are very familiar, which could be your home or a park, etc. The example used here involves moving from the kitchen to the bathroom. You imagine yourself walking past places and items; for example, you start by the fridge, then pass the sink, next the dog's bed, through the kitchen door, into the hall, etc.

You are shopping for your team again and you need:

- frozen peas;
- gravy;
- sausages;
- newspaper;
- apples.

You start at your fridge and notice it has been painted pea green; you walk past the sink, turning on the cold tap, and gravy pours out; as you walk past the dog's bed you see her with a string of sausages wrapped around her neck and one in her mouth; as you walk into the hall someone has covered the floor and walls with newspaper; and as you go to walk up the stairs you are knocked over by a wave of apples hurtling towards you from upstairs.

Forgetting

No matter how well you know something, it is only a matter of time before it is forgotten, but in how much time is up to you. There are a number of things you can do to improve the retention of knowledge.

- Take care to learn it well initially.
- Make links to other knowledge.
- Revisit and revise the knowledge frequently.
- Find out how other people remember things and borrow their techniques.
- Explain to others what you know and how you remember it.
- Reflect on the process of your learning.

Study and learning to study is all about getting to know yourself and finding other ways of doing things. Recognising the type of learners we are will help us to learn and remember. Learning styles are now considered.

The significance of learning styles and memory

Right foot, wrong shoe
People learn in different ways, so what works for one person may not work for another, simply because they think and react very differently. If you are asked to study in a way that you are not used to, it may feel like you are walking in shoes that are just slightly the wrong size. For example, you may be asked to perform mental arithmetic, but you are really much happier using paper and pencil. Often you go about things in a certain way, not because it is the only way you know, but because it is the best for you and the most comfortable. This is not to say that you should not try to learn in new ways, but some-times you know intuitively what is right for you.

Visual, auditory, kinaesthetic
A very general distinction between different types of learners relates to visual (V), auditory (A) and kinaesthetic (K) factors. People are described as having a preference for one of the three ways of learning. Remember, however, that, although you may have a preference, your learning style may well include a VAK combination.

Visually referenced learners rely on sight to make sense of their world. When they learn, they like to see what it is they are learning. For these a diagram, PowerPoint presentation, handout, book, etc. assists their learning. Because the information came into their heads visually, the chances are it will also be recalled visually. When a visually referenced person remembers something, the memory is accessed visually, in other words they may actually see the thing they are remembering. There exist some visual learners who are able to visualise whole pages of text and read them at will. If you are a visual learner, you will see the benefit of both being given the big picture and seeing the fine detail.

REFLECTIVE TASK

Think about your front door – what colour is it? How are you remembering it? Can you see it? Can you see it all or just a part of it? Where in your head are you seeing it? Do you always see things there?

Auditory learners rely on sound to relate to their world. They enjoy listening to others and benefit from sound when learning. They will do well in lectures, as these rely heavily on the spoken word, but, because there is a lot of information contained in the spoken word, auditory learners need to contextualise sounds to trigger memory. For example, think of the ITV *News at Ten*, and now think of the sound of Big Ben. Where do you normally sit when you hear this? Sound can trigger memory in many ways. If you are an auditory learner, you will hear how much sense it makes to study in a way that rings a bell for you. It may be a far cry from some of the learning techniques about which you have heard.

REFLECTIVE TASK

Think about the last time you read a book. When you read the words on the pages, did you hear your own voice even though you were reading to yourself? Alternatively, did you hear the voice of a character depicted in the book? When you read an email from a friend, do you hear their voice in your head? Do you read in perfect silence?

Kinaesthetic learners rely on feelings to relate to their world. Often knowledge is associated with feelings. These can be anywhere on the body and sometimes inside. Kinaesthetic learners prefer activities that involve movement, so to this end a role play would be an appropriate vehicle for learning. Ideas or facts can be placed around parts of the body to assist in learning. The hands are useful for this; here, the hand represents a concept, each finger represents a specific thought and each part of the finger holds a separate strand of information or thought. Space is important to the kinaesthetic learner, and studying in various locations will assist with memory recall by association, for example always studying a particular subject in a particular room. If you are a kinaesthetic leaner you may feel you are getting to grips with this concept and that it is making an impression on you. If you do get the sensation that there is something in it for you, you may be empowered to handle knowledge in this way in future.

REFLECTIVE TASK

Think about the last time you had a physical reaction to something that you read or was said to you. What happened as a result? Ask yourself if you have ever had your heart strings pulled – that is the feeling inside the chest/stomach areas that is associated with a strong emotion. Apparently there are no heart strings inside your body, but that doesn't stop people feeling them.

With VAK in mind, take yourself back to a favourite front door. Do you picture yourself at your door or just see the door itself? Do you hear the sound it makes as it opens or closes? Do you feel yourself releasing the door catch or lock and pushing it open? Think about how you are remembering the features of this door. If you are employing a mixture of VAK, your learning experience and subsequent retrieval of knowledge will be enhanced.

There are numerous learning styles and knowledge of these can be very useful for you; this is because, if you recognise how you best study, you can retrieve the information in an appropriate way. For example, if you were aware that you had a kinaesthetic disposition, placing yourself back in the place where you studied the information will assist retrieval. Likewise, making fantastically coloured and imaginative notes will engage a visual learner's memory. Congruence between the way in which the information was originally placed in the brain and the way in which it is accessed can be very useful in some circumstances; however, as Bloor and Lahiff (2000) pointed out, retrieval is not exclusively dependent on this factor. It may be useful briefly to consider cognitive psychology to better understand how you function when learning.

Revision

Because everyone is different, it is difficult to offer advice to suit all students in every way. However, there are some general principles that will be discussed in this chapter. You can help yourself by considering a few things before you start your revision.

- Which time of the day is best for me to revise?

- Do I need to be uncomfortable or comfortable to be able to concentrate?

- How do I maintain my concentration?

- Do I need to vary my method of revision?

Here are ten principles in relation to revision.

1. Make the process of revision as fun as you can.

2. Tell another person what you can remember about a subject.

3. Break the revision up into short, manageable chunks.

4. Use anything you can to make the information stick: pictures, moving images, tape recordings, etc.

5. Test yourself by setting tasks and writing questions.

6. Do not become distracted.

7. Complete your revision and do not complain about how much you have yet to do.

8. Turn off the phone.

9. Once begun, complete a task.

10. Stay in the here and now.

When to start to prepare for your exam

When you start your course, thoughts of examinations are so far in the future that you will hardly feel the need to give them a passing thought. Exams come at the end of the semester or year and you are at the beginning. The countdown has started and each day of study is a day closer to your exams and some of the subjects you study in the first weeks of your course can find their way into your test papers months later. You should start to prepare for your exams from the very first day of your study. You may remember the Cornell method of note-taking from Chapter 2 (see box overleaf), and following this model will assist in your revision.

2. **Reduce**	1. **Record**
Reduce the original record to concise facts, quotes or questions; these should be in your own words.	Record any facts, phrases, quotes and ideas as fully as is practical.
3. **Recite**	**4 and 5. Reflect and Review**
Covering the original record, recite each fact, quote or question repeatedly.	Reflect on the meaning and correlations of the subject, asking a series of whys.
	Return to these notes frequently over time in order to keep them fresh in your mind.

Conscientious note-taking will ensure that, by the time you come to revise, all the details you require will be close to hand, in order and legible, and will follow a logical/chronological progression. The alternative is not to bother to take notes after about the first two weeks, when you begin to feel at home. The problem here will be that you will then need to revise from the original text. This is achievable but a rather long-winded way to revise. Reflecting on the Cornell method will mean that your revision will be easier because you will have prepared for it well in advance. By the time you begin your revision, you will concern yourself only with parts 3, 4 and 5. Ideally, revision should not be looked at as separate from the learning process, but should be an integral part of it. Revision is really just reminding yourself of the facts, ideas, concepts and theories in relation to your learned subject. If these are not visited frequently, they will gradually be lost.

An organised approach to revision

On a law degree course the subjects included within semester 1 are:

- criminal law;
- contract law;
- access to justice;
- art of persuasion;
- legal systems;
- current legal issues.

Each subject consists of a number of sub-topics, for example the criminal law subjects for semester 1 include:

1. Actus reus;

2. Mens rea;

3. Murder;

4. Manslaughter;

5. Provocation v. diminished responsibility;

6. Duress;

7. Self-defence;

8. Intoxication.

The chart below lists the criminal law subjects as they appear and identifies when each topic should be revised. The numbers on a white background represent the lessons being taught. It is recommended that they are revisited the following week; these revision squares are shaded and become darker the more occasions they are revised. You can see that, over a typical semester of 18 weeks, the earlier subjects may be visited up to six times. However, what should be pointed out is that it is necessary to visit the earlier subjects on more occasions so as not to forget them and, each time a subject is visited, the time spent on the revision should decrease as your ability increases.

Week	Subject							
1	1							
2	2	1						
3	3	2						
4	4	3						
5	5	4	1					
6	6	5	2					
7	7	6	3					
8	8	7	4	1				
9		8	5	2				
10			6	3				
11			7	4	1			
12			8	5	2			
13				6	3			
14				7	4	1		
15				8	5	2		
16					6	3		
17					7	4		
18	3	4	6	7	8	5	2	1

At week 18, all subjects are included prior to the examination. This is only one example of how you may structure your revision. The number of occasions you revisit a topic is dependent upon:

- the difficulty of the topic;

- the percentage of the final mark given to the topic;

- the number of other subjects being studied.

You will notice that, using this model, the revision begins at your second week. Repetition and ensuring that material is left for no more than a month are key to remembering. It does not matter which revision plan you employ; the important thing is that you actually have a plan and stick to it rigidly.

Collating information about the exam

The more information you can glean about the exam you are taking the better, as this will enable you to prepare yourself fully and will ensure that there will be no unwanted surprises. Locate the syllabus for your particular course, as this should indicate the length of each examination and the total marks allocated to it. Identifying what are referred to as the assessment criteria or assessment objectives will enable you to identify exactly what will be expected in relation to the way in which answers are written. Consider the subject content, as this will provide you with the parameters of your study. Lastly, the grade descriptors will provide an indication of what is expected at each grade.

Past papers, if they are available, are always a useful source of information. Never make the mistake of thinking that, just because a topic appeared the previous year, it is unlikely to appear again, as past questions are not indicative of the content of future exams. What they are useful for is guidance on the style and indicative content, how marks are allocated and the style of questions asked.

Another source of useful information to you may be what is called a report on an examination. This analyses how well, or not, the students fared when taking the test and provides examples of both successful and unsuccessful questions. If you are lucky to have access to such a report it will enable you to learn from other students' mistakes.

Ensure that you make yourself aware of any syllabus changes. Liaise with your tutors to this end, as they are there to assist you and it is in their own interest to keep fully up to date with any developments.

It is worth searching the internet for tips and advice, but bear in mind the advice provided in Chapter 6 regarding the quality and reliability of sites. The advice in the following box may be useful to you if you are considering the Bar Exam.

The Bar Exam is divided into eight Bar Subjects spread over four Sundays. While the relative total weights of each of the four Sundays are equal, the eight Bar Subjects are not however of equal weight.

First Sunday			
A.M.:	Political Law & International Law		15%
P.M.:	Labour Law & Social Legislation		10%
		Total	25%
Second Sunday			
A.M.:	Civil Law		15%
P.M.:	Taxation		10%
		Total	25%
Third Sunday			
A.M.:	Mercantile Law		15%
P.M.:	Criminal Law		10%
		Total	25%
Fourth Sunday			
A.M.:	Remedial Law		20%
P.M.:	Legal Ethics & Practical Exercises		5%
		Total	25%

All morning subjects have higher weights compared to the afternoon subjects. Remedial Law is the heaviest (20%) and so it contributes significantly to whether you make it or not. Remedial Law can literally pull you up or down heavily. On the other hand, Legal Ethics & Practical Exercises carries the lightest weight (5%). However, this does not mean that you can take Legal Ethics and Practical Exercises for granted because even if your General Weighted Average is enough to land you in the Top 10, if you get a Grade of lower than 50 in Legal Ethics, you still won't see your name in newspapers or in the Supreme Court website when the results are released.

(Sarmiento, 2009)

The passage in the box above is indicative of how you can benefit from another person's experience or insight. Although all eight subjects are being tested, some are weighted significantly more than others in the allocation of marks. Such things are very useful to be aware of because you will be able to use this knowledge to allocate the amount of time given to each subject.

The allocation of an appropriate proportion of time to a subject is an important consideration. Looking at the Bar Exam chart above for the Fourth Sunday exam, you may be inclined to concentrate 80 per cent of your available time to Remedial Law and the remaining 20 per cent to Legal Ethics & Practical Exercises. However, that not may suit your purposes. Perhaps you are fully conversant with Remedial Law but have neglected Legal Ethics & Practical Exercises. Only you truly know your strengths and weaknesses, so the allocation of time to specific subjects is a matter for your own informed view.

Some frequently asked questions

The following are based upon the Student Information from Greenwich University (2009a).

When will the exams take place? It is highly likely that your college will provide this information within their website. Often universities and colleges hold their examinations in May and January.

How will I know if I have an exam to take? You will be informed by your course tutor or programme leader. Look for any published information in relation to your course. Some colleges enable you to log on to a computer program detailing your course and the related exams, for example BannerWeb (Greenwich University, 2009b).

What do computer programmes such as BannerWeb show you? The list below highlights some of the facilities typically available to students.

- Print coursework header sheets.
- Update your postal addresses.
- Update your email addresses.
- Update your telephone numbers.
- Update your emergency contact information.
- View your financial account.
- Make financial payments.
- View your personal details.
- View details regarding the programme you are studying.
- View details regarding the courses you are studying.
- View your course grades.

How can I access the examination timetable? Normally, this will be accessed via the internet. Looking at the timetable is important as you may find that two of your subjects may be examined at the same time. Checking early will give everyone more time to sort out any issues. Check the timetable on a regular basis as there can often be last-minute changes.

What time do the exams start? Never assume! Just because all the other exams have started at 9.30 a.m. or 2 p.m., this does not mean that they all will. If you are late, you may not be permitted to take the exam. Remember to get there about 15 minutes early.

Where will I take the exam? You can find this information on the exam timetable. Don't assume it will be held in your college; where student numbers are high external venues are hired. If you find that your exam is being held at a venue you have never heard of, find the address, search for it on the computer and go there before the date of the exam. If you are relying on public transport, check the departure and arrival times. If you rely on a car or motorcycle, check for the availability of parking.

Can I telephone the college/university to get my exam dates/times? With the increasing use of the computer as a medium for publishing such information, it is unlikely that the organisation will be willing to offer you information that can easily be found by yourself.

What do I need to bring to the exam? To prevent fraud you will need to bring your ID. If this has been mislaid, another suitable form of identification incorporating a picture may be accepted, such as a driving licence or passport. It is not uncommon for students with no ID to be refused permission to take an exam. You will also need to bring pens/pencils/ruler, etc. Think about how what you do may be perceived, so use a clear pencil case or plastic bag for these items. Don't be upset if these items are checked by invigilators during the exam for any unauthorised material, as this is to protect you from cheats. Ensure that you don't leave any revision notes in your pencil case, etc.; this is easily done, but any notes will be considered as unauthorised material and will be confiscated. You should also bring with you any other items that you are permitted to use for the exam, for example a non-programmable calculator or language dictionary. Remember to ensure that the calculator has new batteries. Again, these will be checked by the invigilator and any unauthorised equipment will be confiscated.

How do I know if I am permitted to use a calculator during the exam? Your course tutor will advise you.

Am I permitted to use a dictionary? Those whose first language is not English can benefit from the use of a dictionary for purposes of translation. However, generally they are not permitted in exams.

Can I bring food and drink into the exam? Water and fruit are sometimes permitted, but be sure to check with your own college/university. Think about the container in which you will place the food, as obviously noisy wrapping should be avoided.

What shall I do with my personal belongings? Take as little as you will require and don't take anything of value with you. Bags, coats and other possessions are not allowed on your desks and are generally placed at the back or side of the room as available.

What about mobile phones? No.

What if I am sick on the day of the exam? Generally, universities/colleges will have an extenuating circumstance form. If you are ill, you must visit your doctor to ask her or him for a note in support of your claim.

What if I am late for the exam? The rules differ, but don't be surprised if you are refused entry. You may be allowed in if you are less than 30 minutes late, but this is at the discretion of the invigilator. In any event, you will not be permitted any extra time because of your late start.

When will I receive my results? A number of things have to occur before you receive your results. The exam papers are marked, and may be moderated and considered by the external moderator from the awarding board. Frequently, the results are published on the internet and posted on a wall in the college/university.

Disability

If you have a disability that will impact upon your ability to take the exam, ensure that you inform the relevant person. Some colleges benefit from the presence of a disability support officer, and you should contact this person or another relevant person as soon as possible for them to make the necessary arrangements for you.

Examination techniques

The more you practise something, generally the better you become at it. This applies as much to exams as to anything else. You may have been studying for a year and feel you know your subject very well indeed, but all that counts is for you to be able to communicate your knowledge to the examiner via the medium of a pen and paper. Exams are not something that people generally enjoy; they worry that they will not be able to answer the questions or that they have not fully prepared. Remember, though, that the only difference between a difficult and an easy question is that you know the answer to the easy one.

You can worry yourself into an inappropriate state, which may not be conducive to your ability to take the exam. Predicting the worst is not helpful, such as imagining yourself on the day of the exam, feeling nervous, having not slept very well the previous night and having missed breakfast. As a result, you imagine yourself feeling light headed and nauseous, and with an awful headache. You predict that, having opened the paper, you arrive at the opinion that exams aren't fair because all that you revised hasn't come up and you are looking at a question paper that, at that moment, you feel may well have been written in a foreign language. Wild imaginings such as this are not helpful because they put you in the wrong frame of mind.

There are things you can do to avoid this undesirable situation; for a start you can begin to think positively about your examination. You have worked hard, so you should not experience too much difficulty answering the questions. The problem some people have is in understanding what the question is actually asking. This can be overcome by studying previous exam papers. If on the day of the exam you don't understand the question, ask the invigilator, who may be able to assist you.

You should practise for your exam by sitting through examination conditions. Other than practising with previous exam papers, another useful technique is to write your own questions and then answer them; this will provide you with a huge insight into how the examiners compose the questions. There will be a limited number of questions that can be written about a subject, and you could even find that one of your own questions comes up in the exam. Practice at answering questions will enable you to identify your own cognitive recall, and will also enable you to practise answering questions precisely and within a limited time frame.

Examination tips

Before the exam starts

- Make sure you are registered for the exam.

- Before the exam, find out how much time the exam paper has been allocated. Do not wait until the day of the exam to do this; you can do this weeks in advance; ask your tutor or contact the examining board directly.

- Compare this allocated time to your syllabus and ensure you have identified exactly what subject areas are likely to be tested.

- On the day of the exam, eat breakfast and ensure that you are fully hydrated.

- Check the college/university website to ensure that there have been no last-minute changes to times and locations.

- Make sure you have all you need, including a map and ID if necessary.

- Leave in plenty of time, as you don't want to be stuck on a bus when the exam is starting.

- Don't try and cram as much revision as possible into your head before the exam. This will just panic you, as you will convince yourself of how much you have forgotten or simply don't know.

- Avoid discussing the topic with others just before the exam, as again it may panic you.

- Believe in yourself and walk into the examination room in the knowledge that, with all the hard work and study you have completed, you will do well.

Before you start writing

- Read the instructions relating to the exam carefully.

- Make sure you have identified exactly how many questions you should be answering.

- Read the questions slowly.

- Read the questions again, as this will negate any effect of nervousness.

- Don't panic if you are unable to understand or answer a question. Go to the next question and then return to the difficult one later.

- Answer the questions you think you can answer best first, where there is a choice.

- Answer the questions you have been asked rather than the questions you wanted.

- Use the marks allocated to each question to guide the amount of time you should spend on each.

- Plan your time to leave enough time to check work.

- Consider how you will set out your answer sheet as your answers need to be legible.

During the exam

- Make sure you have the correct exam paper. If you think you may not, then ask.

- Make sure you have pens, spare pens, pencils and, if you are using a calculator, a battery that will last for the duration of the exam.

- Read through the paper from start to finish. Identify the questions that you can do easily and those that you will find a little harder. Allocate an appropriate amount of time to each question, remembering to check the allocation of marks. Give the most time to those with the most marks allocated.

- You do not always have to work through the questions in the order in which they appear. However, some knowledge and reasoning types of question may rely on the knowledge from a previous scenario being drawn into following questions, so be sure to identify this.

- If you are really stuck, leave the question and go back to it later, which will give your brain time to work it out for you while you occupy yourself with other questions. Look for clues – if there are three marks allocated, it may be that they are looking for three facts.

- RTQ! Read the question! Take, for example, these instructions from the London School of Economics (2009): 'Candidates should answer **FOUR** of the following **EIGHT** questions: **ONE** from Section A, **ONE** from Section B, and **TWO** further questions from either section. All questions carry equal marks.' If you do not follow the instructions, although you may have answered the questions correctly, as you have not answered the correct questions, you will receive no marks.

- Answer all the questions, as you cannot get a mark for writing nothing. If you guess, you have lost nothing and you may get the answer partially correct.

- Try to keep your writing neat and tidy. It may feel like you are being tested on your ability to write quickly and your hand may be aching. However, remember the poor person who has to mark your work. If they cannot read the answer, you will get no marks.

- If you make a mistake, don't panic – deal with it.

- Leave a little time at the end of the exam to read over and correct your work where necessary.

When you have finished the exam

- Go back to the beginning and check the questions. Ask yourself, 'Have I answered the question?' If not, then add to your answers.

- Check for spelling mistakes and grammatical errors.

- As you read, ask yourself if you have said what it was you intended to say.

- Check your answers; are they complete or have you missed parts of the question?

- Do your answers match the question, or have you become confused?

- If you have been taking a multiple-choice test, if you have missed out one question, has this now put all your answers out of sync?

- Resist the temptation to read too much into a question and assume. The authors' observations have shown that student police officers frequently change a correct answer to an incorrect one.

- If you have time, read the paper over again to ensure that nothing has been over-looked.

- Do not leave the room early; make the best use of your time.

- Know when to stop.

After the exam

- Don't worry about the exam you have just sat, as it is over and you cannot change what has been done.

- Don't talk to other candidates about their answers to specific questions; all that matters is what you have done.

- If you feel there were circumstances that affected your performance in any way, ensure that you discuss it there and then and that your conversation is recorded.

- Don't dwell on imagined past performances; you will not know how you did until the results are published.

- Focus on your next exam.

Writing style

Different subjects require specific writing styles; for example, you will find the style for a psychology paper will differ significantly from that of a law paper. Your reading, writing and feedback from your tutor will contribute to the style of writing you adopt. During the exam there are a number of dos and don'ts to consider. For example, it is not necessary for you to rewrite the question into your answer paper. To identify it all that is necessary is to label it, so if your answer relates to the second question, part b, it would be appropriate to write Q2 (b) clearly next to your answer. Where a question asks a number of questions, separate them out and deal with each part in turn. Make sure you employ the use of appropriate sentences, rather than a shorthand response that could be misinterpreted. If your response requires the use of a list, bullet point the list for ease of reading, but beware of making your entire response a collection of bullet points; use them sparingly.

Always keep in mind the person who will be marking your paper. Where you have changed a response, ensure that the incorrect answer is clearly crossed out without making a terrible mess. Where you have made notes, distinguish between these and your actual answer. Remember, you are trying to communicate with the person marking your paper, so help them as much as you are able. There is no mark for being neat and, equally, there are no marks for things that can't be read. How much you write is a matter for you and your exam technique, but be guided by the question and the allocation of marks. For example, if you are asked to describe something briefly, a tome of the magnitude of War and Peace will not be expected.

CHAPTER SUMMARY

In this chapter we have identified the principles of memory and have described some strategies for remembering facts. We have also pointed out the relationship between learning styles and memory. Appropriate revision techniques were then described, including preparing for your exam and organising your revision, and we stressed the importance of collating information about the exam. Finally, we have presented some exam techniques and tips and have pointed out the importance of adopting an appropriate writing style in your examination.

REFERENCES

Bloor, M and Lahiff, A (2000) *Perspectives on Learning: A Reader.* London: Greenwich University Press

Gould, J (2009). *Learning Theory and Classroom Practice in the Lifelong Learning Sector.* Exeter: Learning Matters.

Greenwich University (2009a) *Student Information*. Available online at www.gre.ac.uk/students/exams/frequently-asked-questions (accessed 10 December 2009)

Greenwich University (2009b) *BannerWeb Information.* Available online at www.greenwich.ac.uk/bannerinfo/bannerWebforStudent/ (accessed 10 December 2009).

London School of Economics and Political Science (2009) LSE External Study: Format of examination papers in 2009. Available online at www2.lse.ac.uk/study/ExternalStudy/ExamNotice2009exams.pdf (accessed 10 December 2009)

Sarmiento, RA (2009) *Bar Exam Tips & Secrets*. Available online at http://attyralph.com/BarTips/1.Subjects_and_Schedules.html (accessed 10 December 2009).

9 The research project

Introduction

In most foundation degree and degree courses you are required to conduct a research project of some considerable length. This is usually in the final year of your studies, either alongside studying other modules or after you have completed those modules. You work on your research project independently, but you will be allocated a supervisor to guide and support you. This chapter explains what is meant by research, describing different approaches to research, the theoretical perspectives and methodologies. It guides you in choosing a topic for you to research and explains how to conduct a literature review and how to collect and analyse data. Further, it discusses ethical considerations and specifies the role of the supervisor.

To ensure that the use of research results is maximised, they must be disseminated in an appropriate manner, usually in the form of a dissertation. The dissertation is just as important as the research activity itself and will be discussed in Chapter 10.

The whole process may seem scary at the moment – a daunting task. However, in simple terms, all it means is: ask a question, find the answer and report your findings.

What is research?

Research is about finding out, and is a systematic investigation and discovery by testing hypotheses and ideas. It is what we do if there is a question, or maybe a problem, that we want to resolve. The outcome of research is new knowledge, leading to improved understanding and the development of new and improved procedures. In other words, the purpose of research is to 'gather and analyse appropriate evidence on which to base decisions to bring about change' (Burton et al., 2008, p17). Sometimes the answer can seem obvious or perhaps you have a 'gut-feeling' as to what the answer is. However, you need systematically and rigorously to research the situation to prove this gut feeling, while keeping an open mind if the results are different and not in line with your expectations.

PRACTICAL TASK

What research has recently been published by the Home Office?

Look at 'Publications' on the Home Office web page, Research Development Statistics: www.homeoffice.gov.uk/rds/.

Approaches to research

There are different approaches to research. One of those approaches, or methodologies, is the traditional scientific method of investigation. This is referred to as the objective or 'positivist' approach. The term 'positivism' is credited to the French philosopher, Auguste Comte, during the Industrial Revolution. Objective researchers, or positivists, believe that facts exist 'out there'; their research merely uncovers those facts. They use methods that allow for the collection of large amounts of quantitative (numerical) data, but with limited personal involvement, staying on the outside, keeping the research value-free. They generalise from these data, looking for trends and patterns and, from this, seek universally applicable rules and laws. Positivists look for correlations, so, when two or more things are found together, they look for the strength of the relationship between those things.

Positivist research also involves a search for causal connections: when two phenomena are found together, can it be proven that one causes the other? However, one has to be careful when drawing such conclusions. Haralambos and Holborn (1995) give the following example. Many sociologists have noted a correlation between being working class and having a relatively high chance of being convicted of a crime. This has led some to speculate that being working class is one factor that might cause people to commit criminal acts: 'being working class causes crime'. However, there are many other possibilities that might explain the correlation, so it cannot be concluded that crime is a result of being working class. Further, positivists prove or disprove hypotheses, carry out experiments and conduct surveys.

A second approach is that of 'interpretivism', also referred to as anti-positivism, which explores people's feelings and emotions, and how they think and see themselves. Researchers interpret their actions and make sense of the situation. The emphasis in interpretive research, as used by its founder, Max Weber (1863–1931), is on 'verstehen' (to understand). The aim of research is to see the world through the eyes of those involved. Data collected are qualitative in nature, dealing with depth and detail and words, quotes and observations rather than numbers. The researcher interprets the findings and forms an integral part of the research, bringing his or her own values into it. Interpretive research is therefore subjective in nature.

Interpretivists criticise positivists for seeing patterns where they may not exist, for instance by generalising from statistics. They argue that these so-called facts are social constructions of the researchers who put those statistics together, and interpreted them, in the first place. Positivists, on the other hand, criticise interpretive research, because, although it may be valid, it lacks reliability, therefore making it difficult to generalise from it. In reality, the divide between the two methodologies, positivism and interpretivism, is not so clear, as, on occasion, the only way to get a fuller picture is to mix methods, producing both quantitative and qualitative data. Mixed methods are often used in case-study research, in which one case, with well-defined boundaries in terms of participants, location, organisation and time, is studied in detail. Although the case study is often classified as qualitative by definition, quantitative methods and data can be appropriate. However, you should base your approach to research on the best way to get an answer to your question.

A third type of research is 'action research', also referred to as participatory research. The emphasis is on improving your practice. In this style, the researcher identifies a problem, intervenes by making changes (which is the action) and measures the effects. The work of Kurt Lewin (1946), who researched social issues, has been described as a 'major landmark in the development of action research as a methodology' (Koshy, 2005, p2). The advantages of action research are that it is participatory, as the researchers can also be participants; it is set in a specific situation, involving researching your own practice; and, as it involves continuous evaluation, you can make modifications throughout the project. Overall, action research can be 'real-life' problem-solving. However, there are also limitations, as it can be considered to lack rigour and validity; you cannot make generalisations from the research; and there is even 'the chance that work may degenerate into haphazard tinkering' (Swetnam, 2000, p36).

Which approach would you take to find out the following?

- *An exploration of the experiences of community support officers on a local council estate.*

- *The effects of community support officers on anti-social behaviour.*

(The answer is given at the end of the chapter.)

Choosing an area of research

This is the first and one of the most important decisions you make. As stated by Currie, 'Everything you do, from deciding on your approach to the type of data you collect, is determined by the nature of the topic you choose' (2005, p110). The aim is to move away from a wide area of interest or concern to a specific question. You may have some ideas already, but you can use the following techniques to develop possible issues for research.

- Talk to people and exchange ideas.

- Think of what issues have interested you through your place of work or through the news, or that have been raised by colleagues.

- What arguments, controversies and discussions have you heard about policing recently?

- Think about innovations and policies that affect your work.

Once you have made a decision on a topic, check it against the following checklist (adapted from Currie, 2005).

- **Relevance**: Is the subject relevant to a discipline that is within the main syllabus of your course?

- **Interest**: As you will be spending a lot of time on the subject, it is important that you are interested in it; better still, are passionate about it. If not, you might become bored and fed up with the topic.

- **Familiarity**: Do not choose something expecting an easy ride. Although, on the one hand, it is beneficial to research something you are already familiar with, on the other hand, it may be restricting. Maybe you try to upgrade something you have done before, but this may be problematic as the new research does not quite fit in with your previous work.

- **Researchability**: Trawl the literature, identifying the breadth and depth of the available relevant reading. Will you be given permission by relevant bodies to carry out the research?

- **Capability**: Consider the skills involved in carrying out the research. For instance, if you decide to do an experiment or survey, how are you with statistics; can you work out standard deviations, etc.?

- **Feasibility**: Is it possible to carry out the research within the allocated time, within a particular budget, etc.?

The idea is to keep your research really focused. The main problem often is that students choose an area of research that is far too wide for the number of words they are allocated for the dissertation and the time frame within which they have to work. A longitudinal study, on some occasions taking years, may be very interesting and worthwhile but will not be feasible for your research project.

Literature review

Before you can start your actual research you need to gather information about the topic, reading what has already been found out to provide a background. This is referred to as the 'literature search'. However, rather than just listing what other people have said about the topic, for a review of the literature you need to analyse, compare and contrast other people's views and ideas. This demonstrates that you are familiar with what has already been done and are aware of the latest developments and their impacts.

Where do you start? A trip to the library or LRC may be required. In your literature you need to be selective; however, it may take some time and reading to decide what you want to use. You can select from books, journals or from the internet, but make sure the references you use are from reputable sources. When reading a publication it is helpful to look at the references the author has used. It may be that these references can guide you for your own reading. When you come across something that might be useful for your argument, make sure you make a note of its exact location by referencing accurately.

You need some sort of filing strategy. Some people use cards on which they write the quote, filing them in alphabetical order by the name of the author; others file them according to themes. Another way is to photocopy the page on which you have found the useful quote and highlight it, again making a note of the author, publication, date of publication, etc. Alternatively, you can use the computer to manage your findings. The main point is to keep your readings accessible, as it can be very frustrating and time consuming to search for a citation that you know must be somewhere in your pile of paperwork, but where . . .?

When to stop reading is another difficult decision, as you could probably carry on forever. As a general rule, you have probably exhausted the literature when you start reading the same things over and over again. Also, once you start recognising where other authors are quoting from, you have probably read enough.

Next, you need to put your findings together in a cohesive manner with a logical structure. It is best to write a draft first, checking that you have gathered sufficient information and that you understand the ideas of other experts in the field, taking a critical approach. Further, it is important to use in your review only what is purposeful to your argument. You may be tempted to use quotes just to show your tutors that you have read far more. However, random quotes, taking you off track, do not support your argument. It is best to accept that you will be reading more in your literature review than you will use, even if you keep it as focused as possible. All reading contributes to your wider knowledge and understanding and, therefore, is not wasted. To check for any gaps, inconsistencies or off-track comments, Currie offers a useful tip:

When you have drafted a copy of your literature review, read it aloud to yourself. It is surprising how this will help you to sort out any clumsy, ill-written or muddled phrasing.

(2005, p81)

Once you are satisfied with the content of your literature review, check it for accuracy on citing and referencing, as failing to do so may result in an allegation of plagiarism, which, as discussed earlier in the book, is regarded as a serious offence. When completed, your literature review should:

- provide a context for the research;

- demonstrate that you are familiar with the topic;

- analyse, compare and contrast what others have said on the topic;

- provide evidence to support your argument, taken from reputable sources;

- show where your research fits into the main body of knowledge.

Methods of data collection

How you collect your data very much depends on which approach you have taken in your research design. Positivist researchers collect data from experiments, surveys, closed questionnaires and highly structured interviews, whereas interpretivist researchers make more use of observation, semi-structured or unstructured interviews or open-ended questionnaires. In other words, positivists work with quantitative data, such as statistics, and interpretivists with qualitative data.

Experiments

In its purest form the experiment method is principally associated with the 'physical sciences'. Hypotheses, based on observation or theory, are formulated and tested, proving the hypothesis to be right or not. The whole process is characterised by precision, accurate measurement and duplication, which should enable exact prediction and generality (Swetnam, 2000). Experiments in social sciences are more difficult to control and there may be some ethical issues. In general, the experiment is based on comparisons between two groups. In the simplest case, the researcher will do something to one group, the experimental group, while not changing the other, the control group. In all other aspects the groups should be alike, the only difference being the intervention or treatment they receive.

The term 'variables' is often used: the 'independent variable' is what the researcher does to the experimental group (the researcher manipulates the independent variable), and this manipulation can be considered as the cause; next, a comparison is made between the experimental group and the control group. The difference in outcome is the 'dependent variable', or the effect. Therefore, in experimental research you must distinguish between the independent variables – those that are manipulated by the researcher, and the dependent variables – those that change as a result of the manipulation.

A challenge in experimental research is to set up a control group that is as similar as possible, in all respects, to the experimental group, ensuring that the only difference is the exposure to the independent variable. You can try deliberately matching each group member, in terms of relevant characteristics. However, this quickly runs into problems, as finding an exact match for each member may be hard to achieve. A more common approach is to assign participants randomly to the control group. Punch (2009, p217) points out that, although the random assignment of participants to control groups does not guarantee alikeness or equality between the comparison groups, it does maximise the probability that they will not differ in any systematic way. He goes on to summarise a true experiment as:

- the manipulation of one or more independent variables for the purpose of research, and

- the random assignment of participants to comparison groups.

REFLECTIVE TASK

Read up on the Stanford Prison Experiment, which you can access on www.apa.org/ research/action/prison.aspx or www.prisonexp.org/legnews.htm.

The first of these sites states:

> *In 1971, a team of psychologists designed and executed an unusual experiment that used a mock prison setting, with college students role-playing prisoners and guards to test the power of the social situation to determine behavior.*

- *What are your thoughts on carrying out experiments on people?*

- *What are the advantages and disadvantages?*

Surveys

Surveys gather information from a large group of people, or population. As you cannot contact everybody within that population, it is common practice to select a sample, or cross-section, of people drawn from that population. As pointed out by Currie:

> A survey is a technique in which a sample of prospective respondents is selected from a population. The sample is then studied with a view to drawing inferences from their responses to the statements in a questionnaire, or the questions in a series of interviews.

(2005, p94)

This method may seem easy, and maybe because of that is popular with students. Disappointingly, the response rate to surveys is often very low. Respondents may not be motivated to reply or are irritated by the whole thing: how many times have you discarded one of those 'national' surveys without even looking at it – or maybe just rescuing the free pen! Further, how can you be sure that the respondents have understood and interpreted the questions correctly; how do you know they have not merely lied, for the fun of it?

When choosing the survey method you have to be careful how to determine your sample: is it representative and is it large enough to be significant (the smaller the sample, the less you can generalise from it)? However, there is no definite answer as to how large your sample should be. You have to make a judgement, weighing the representativeness against, for instance, the costs of contacting a large number of people (time, postage, telephone costs, etc.).

The strategies for selecting a sample from a population fall into two categories: probability sampling and non-probability sampling. Probability sampling is commonly used if the sample size is large. Strategies include:

- random sampling; large random samples are best computer generated;

- systematic sampling, by selecting each nth person from a list;

- stratified sampling, in which a layer is selected;

- cluster sampling, in which groups are defined by area or geographical region.

Non-probability sampling is commonly used if the sample is smaller or where bias is not considered to be an issue. Strategies include:

- opportunity sampling; perhaps you have access to a certain group of officers and can ask them to participate;

- volunteer sampling, which is allowing people to come forward themselves;

- purpose or judgemental sampling, which is handpicking those you want to include in your sample.

An advantage of survey research is that, on the one hand, you can potentially gather a lot of data from even a small number of participants. On the other hand, small-scale surveys may lack depth.

Questionnaires

Questionnaires are one of the most commonly used methods of data collection. They are used to collect straightforward information, but can also be used to explore views, opinions and perceptions. Questionnaires are structured, unstructured or semi-structured. This means that they use closed questions, open questions, or a combination of closed and open questions. Structured questionnaires tend to be used for larger samples and are easier to analyse, as you only have to deal with tick-box responses. Unstructured questionnaires are unsuitable for large samples as they need more time to analyse.

REFLECTIVE TASK

What are your thoughts on the following questionnaire?

Questionnaire

1. *Title (circle)*

    Mr   Mrs   Other

2. *Age group (circle)*

    20–30   30–40   40–50   50–60

3. *How long have you been a police officer/community support officer?*

    years   months

4. *Like most people, do you hate doing night shifts?*

    Yes/No

5. *Do you agree with the concept of NDNAD?*

    Yes/No

6. *Marital status (circle)*

    Single   Married   Divorced   Civil partnership

7. *No police officer should have to be accurate in their original notes.*

    Agree/Disagree

8. *Are your parents and children proud of your achievements as a police officer/community support officer?*

    Yes/No

9. *In your own words (500), what do you think of the way crime is reported?*

You may have queried the purpose of the questionnaire in the last task, finding it hard to answer all questions. This highlights that the design of a questionnaire has to be carefully considered. First, you need to be clear about the purpose of the data you need in relation to your research question. What exactly do you want to find out? Is it relevant to ask for participants' age and marital status? On occasion, researchers ask too many irrelevant questions, as they wonder whether they may need such information at a later stage; will it be significant for their research after all? As a rule, consider how many questions are necessary and order them in a logical sequence. Remember, you are taking your participants' time, so be careful not to waste it. Therefore, avoid:

*   leading questions (such as question 4 in the questionnaire);
*   complexity; two questions in one (questions 3, 8);

- negatives and double negatives, as they lead to confusion (question 7);
- jargon (question 5, National DNA Database);
- ambiguity (questions 2, 9);
- irritating questions (questions 1, 6: options limited; question 9: too time-consuming; all questions: how are they relevant?).

As mentioned before, closed questions are easier to analyse (imagine analysing the responses if you send question 9 to 100 participants!). Although, arguably, you get more in-depth responses from open questions, by introducing more options for your participants to choose from, you can get more detailed information. Here are some examples.

- **Multiple choice**

  Tick one of the following:

  A Crime always pays   ❑

  B Crime may pay   ❑

  C Crime never pays   ❑

  D Crime costs   ❑

- **Rating scale (Likert scale)**

  Circle the number that most accurately reflects your feelings.

  'All first offenders of shoplifting should be given a warning only'

  1. strongly agree   2. agree   3. disagree   4. strongly disagree

  Another example:

  How do you rate the cleanliness of your station?

Very poor				Very good
1	2	3	4	5

- **Ranking**

  Order according to importance 1–5 (1 very important; 5 not important)

  Approachability of front counter staff   ❑

  Waiting time before seen   ❑

  Efficiency of front counter staff   ❑

  Opening times of station   ❑

  Interpersonal skills of counter staff   ❑

It is strongly recommended that you pilot your questionnaire first, before using it, as this will identify any ambiguous or unclear questions. Make sure that the layout of the questionnaire is clear and that you keep to the same format. Most people prefer ticking a box or circling an answer, while few bother to write comments. Further, as with a survey, the response rate to postal questionnaires is usually low and you don't know who completed the questionnaire. Always explain the purpose of the questionnaire to your participants, either in the heading or in an accompanying letter.

Interviews

The interview is sometimes described as a 'conversation with a purpose'. It is a flexible way of collecting data, which are usually more in-depth and richer, adding to the validity of the research. An advantage of interviews is that people are more easily engaged in an interview than in completing a questionnaire. Before conducting an interview you need to consider how you will record the responses. Will you make notes or ask someone else to make notes, or will you record the interview using a Dictaphone or tape recorder? Whichever method you decide on, make sure you use it with the participant's consent. There are different types of interviews: structured, unstructured or semi-structured. Further, as well as individual interviews, you can consider conducting a group interview, a focus group interview or even telephone or videoconference interviews.

Structured interviews

In a structured interview the researcher reads out a set of specified, closed questions. Every participant is asked the same questions in the same order. This makes it very easy to compare results. Recording the responses only requires a tick in a box or one-word answer, resulting in more quantitative data.

The design of the interview questions raises the same issues as the design of a questionnaire: they need to be clear, not ambiguous, not leading, etc. If the structure is very rigid it can be argued that you might as well do a questionnaire. The advantage, however, of an interview is that the participant can ask the interviewer to repeat the question or ask for some clarification. A disadvantage is that there is more chance of bias, as the interviewer can emphasise certain words or phrases, even adapting their body language.

Semi-structured interviews

In a semi-structured interview the questions are usually specified, but they tend to be more open-ended or a mix of closed and open questions. The interviewer can follow up any questions with prompting or probing, seeking clarification and elaboration. The participant can talk more freely and expand upon answers. The interviewer has to be careful managing this. On the one hand, the extra information adds to the depth and richness of the data, as you get more information. On the other hand, there is a chance of digressing, losing the focus of the interview.

Recording the responses yourself by making notes may interrupt the flow of the interview, as you will lose eye contact as you look down to write the responses and you may not be able to record everything. Relying on your memory and recording the responses afterwards may not always be appropriate, as it is easy to forget the exact reply. You can consider someone else doing the recording but this means an extra person in the room, which may put pressure on the participant; further, can you rely on someone else, as they probably 'hear' things differently from you, adding their own interpretation? A recording device may be the best way. Although they can be off-putting at first, participants usually get used to recorders quickly, forgetting that they are there. You must get consent from the participant and explain to them where data are kept (in a locked drawer) and what you will do with the data once the research has been completed (tapes are usually destroyed). Data from these interviews are harder to analyse, as they tend to be qualitative in nature.

Unstructured interviews

In the unstructured interview you are more a facilitator than an interviewer. You decide on the subject for the interview, an open-ended question, but the participant is in control of how the interview develops. The main advantage of an unstructured interview is that it allows you to probe in even greater depth, resulting in rich information from the participant. Writing down responses yourself is totally inappropriate, so your best option is to record the interview. Transcribing and analysing the data can be a lengthy process. Consider this before you decide on the number of participants you wish to interview. The more structured the interview, the easier the analysis, so the more people you can interview.

Group or focus group interviews

To save yourself time, it may be appropriate to conduct a group or focus group interview. They are efficient in the sense that they generate large quantities of material from relatively large numbers of people in a relatively short time. Participants are selected because they have certain characteristics in common, relating to the topic of the interview. However, this type of interview may be harder to organise, as you deal with more people, and you have to consider whether people will talk freely in the presence of others.

As with the unstructured interview, your role is to guide the conversation, keeping it to the theme. Keeping control can be hard, as people have conversations among themselves, talk over each other or don't finish their sentences. Further, the chance of straying off track is substantial, as one thing leads to another. However, this may give you far richer data, as participants probe each other's reasons for holding a view. Transcribing the interview requires some skill, as it can be difficult to ascertain who said what and how it was said. How do you record several mini-conversations, some whispered, some taking place at the same time, etc.?

Telephone interviews and videoconferencing

The results of telephone interviews can be mixed. As with the other types of interview it is best to arrange a suitable time rather than phoning unannounced. Have you ever put the phone down when contacted around tea-time to answer some questions on shopping habits, insurance, mobile phones or overdrafts? These phone calls can be annoying, so make sure yours isn't one of them. The overall effectiveness is highest when the interview is structured and lowest when unstructured, as opportunities for prompting and probing are limited when you can't see the other person.

Videoconferencing overcomes this problem to a certain extent, although it still isn't the same as talking to someone in the same room. An advantage of telephone and videoconference interviews is that you can interview people living too far away for you to interview face to face, thereby widening your sample and ensuring that you interview people who can really contribute to the subject you are researching.

General guidance on conducting interviews

- Arrange a time and place convenient to the participant(s).

- Be prepared: questions, recording method, etc.

- Pilot the interview.

- Dress appropriately for the occasion: power-dressing may be off-putting; overly casual wear may appear unprofessional.

- Be friendly, yet formal and build a rapport with your participants.

- Inform participants of the purpose of the interview and explain what will be done with the data afterwards.

- Do not make assumptions.

- Do not volunteer answers or complete people's sentences.

- Avoid innuendo or irony.

- Be non-judgemental.

- Stick to the time schedule.

- Thank your participants for their time and contributions.

Observation

Although less frequently used than surveys or interviews, observing your participants in their 'natural setting' is another way of collecting data. The researcher watches and listens to the participants rather than asking questions. There are two main ways of doing this: as a participant or as a non-participant observer.

Participant observation

As a participant, the researcher is part of the group that is being observed, becoming involved with the participants and their activities. You record what you see, writing notes or diaries. Data are therefore qualitative in nature.

One of the disadvantages of observation techniques is that of response bias. People may act differently if they know they are being observed. Over time they may become used to your presence, forgetting what you're doing, but that means spending a lot of time with the group, which is time you may not have. On occasion, research has been carried out where the researchers have not explained what they were doing, carrying out 'covert' research by infiltrating an organisation or group and pretending to be one of them, but secretly observing its members (remember 'fly on the wall' series?). Although your data may be more valid, as the participants behave more naturally, questions need to be asked about whether it is ethical to carry out such research.

A further issue is that of observer bias. It is very unlikely that two observers notice and record exactly the same things, as they will interpret what they see differently. This may affect the outcome of the research: two observers, in the same setting, can produce different reports of their findings. Also, as no two groups or two natural settings are alike, it is difficult to make comparisons.

Analysing the data from the notes you have taken can be very time-consuming and relies on further interpretation. This type of research is not usually considered to be reliable.

Non-participant observation

The non-participant observer does not take part in the activities and is not considered to be a member of the group. There is still the issue of response bias, whereby the participants do what they think the observer wants them to do, thus skewing the data. On occasion, observing from behind a one-way mirror may be considered, although, unless there is a very good reason for doing this, it does not appear ethical without the participants' knowledge. Techniques for recording what you see include taking notes; keeping a tally chart, recording how often specific actions or interactions take place; interval sampling, recording what is going on at specific time intervals; and photographing or filming the participants.

To limit observer bias, thereby increasing reliability of the research, you can design an observation schedule, structuring what you are looking for. This focuses the observation on certain behaviours or interactions and ensures that it is more likely that different researchers will observe the same. Data from this type of observation are more quantitative in nature and easier to analyse (for instance, A interacted x times with B).

Secondary data

The methods of data collection discussed so far result in giving you primary data. On occasion it might be useful to research an already existing body of data, such as other research results, annual reports and other documentary analysis. This is referred to as 'desktop research'. The advantages of this type of research are that it is low in cost and time-efficient, and makes difficult populations accessible. A disadvantage, however, is that the original questions and data may not be entirely relevant to your research question. Therefore, you have to be very careful in planning this type of research.

An overview of data-collection methods is given in Table 9.1.

Table 9.1 *Methods of data collection overview*

Method	Type	Advantage	Disadvantage
Experiment	Comparison between two groups	Reliable, valid, generalisable	Ethical considerations
Survey	Survey	Gathers lots of information; easy to administer and analyse	Sampling can be an issue and this may affect validity, reliability, generalising; low response rate
Questionnaire	Structured; unstructured; semi-structured; rating scales (Likert); ranking	Quick; structured questionnaires can reach a large sample; easy to analyse; researcher doesn't have to be present	Can be difficult to design; data lack depth; questions cannot be explained; no prompting or probing; possibly low response
Interview	Unstructured; semi-structured; structured; group/focus group; telephone	Flexible way of collecting data; usually high in validity; depth of data; can be followed up; prompting and probing; relatively easy to construct	Time consuming; the less structured the interview the less reliable it becomes; interviewer bias; recording; analysis
Observation	Participant; non-participant	High in validity; richness of data	Response bias; observer bias; not always reliable; difficult to generalise from; ethical issues to consider
Secondary data	Documents, previous research	Low in cost; time-efficient; can make difficult populations accessible	Data may be not be entirely relevant to current research

Data analysis

Once you have collected your data, you need to make sense of them: how will you analyse the completed questionnaires, transcripts of interviews, notes and/or observations? Sharp puts it succinctly: 'take apart what you have, examine it in detail, and put it all back together again in a more condensed and meaningful way' (2009, p103).

The first step is to make sure that you know exactly what information you have got, familiarising yourself with it. Next, you reduce the data, organising it into smaller chunks, perhaps by topic, category or theme (you can use a coding system for this). From this, you may identify some patterns or relationships, which you can compare to the literature. The raw data now become 'findings' that you can interpret and comment on. It may be appropriate to present your findings in tables or, more visually, in graphs or charts. However, be careful to use this only when it is meaningful, as pretty coloured graphs, etc., can easily lead to overkill. If you do use tables and graphs it is helpful to the reader of your project to give each a title, rather than referring to, say, table 1 or graph 1 only.

Quantitative data are analysed by using statistics. This means you have to be fairly skilled in mathematics, being able to work out percentages but also averages (mean, mode and median) and maybe standard deviations (measuring the spread of the data about the mean value). Consider this before you embark on large-scale survey research (although there are computer software packages available, such as SPSS and Minitab, to assist you).

Purely descriptive qualitative data can be difficult to present. Swetnam (2000) recommends that they need careful editing and benefit from being presented in blocks, broken up with subtitles.

Reliability, validity and generalisability

'These three concepts help provide blunt answers to the questions: Is the research any good; is it of use?' (Swetnam, 2000, p29).

Research is reliable if it can be reproduced; that is, if the same procedures or actions, if carried out again, would lead to the same results.

Research is valid if it measures what we claim it to measure. Further, can we generalise from it; is the research applicable to other situations? Traditionally, positivist or quantitative research claims all three, but it is easy to be impressed by figures and statistics. Swetnam (2000) refers to this as the 'lure of numbers', which he explains as an unjustified belief that data involving measurement are more valuable than things that are observed or described. It is therefore important that the qualitative researcher subjects all data to rigorous examination. One way of doing this is to employ more than one method of data collection in the same study, which allows you the opportunity to cross-check your findings. This technique is referred to as 'triangulation'; for example, you glean information from questionnaires that you check by carrying out some interviews.

Ethical considerations

Ethics are a vital part of research. First, you must make sure that you have been given permission to have access to the participants. Next, it is essential that you inform your participants of the purpose of the research and gain their informed consent. This may be in the form of a 'consent' sheet, where the participant signs that they have given their consent to taking part in the research. You must also ensure that participants can withdraw from taking part in the research at any point, or withdraw their data from the research, if they change their minds.

No harm must come to your participants by taking part in the research and it may be courteous to inform them of the end result. You need to explain where data will be stored and what will happen to the data once the research has been completed. It goes without saying that confidentiality will be adhered to throughout the process. This means you have to be careful not to use participants' real names, or possibly their place of work, thus protecting their identity, as otherwise it might be easy to trace them back.

Further, there may be a 'power' issue to consider. If you are part of the same organisation, especially if you are higher in rank, participants may feel they have to participate, as they may fear repercussions if they don't. You need to be aware of the fact that they might only tell you what they think you will want to hear, thus skewing the data.

The role of the supervisor

Your tutor, or maybe someone else from the teaching team, will be allocated to be your supervisor for the duration of the research project or dissertation. Your supervisor offers guidance and advice whenever appropriate, as he or she is usually an expert in the field and can recommend appropriate reading, including other research. That is why a supervisor is usually allocated after you have chosen a subject for your research. It may be useful to find out how many hours are allocated to supervision and the best time and method to contact your supervisor.

It is important that you maintain a good relationship with your supervisor and that you stay in touch. Especially if you work independently, after completing the other modules on the programme, it is crucial that you keep informing your supervisor of your progress. Or, if you are stuck on something and not making the expected progress, you will need to discuss a way forward. Although supervisors will endeavour to keep in touch with you, it is worth remembering that, ultimately, the responsibility lies with you, the student. It is your work that is assessed, not that of the supervisor.

Supervisors normally accept drafts of parts of the dissertation and provide feedback. It is not always necessary to meet face to face, as on occasion drafts can be sent by email. Supervisors may give feedback in general, or they can make use of 'Track changes' as found under 'Tools' on your computer. This way, your supervisor can make comments and suggest changes that you can accept or not. If at all possible, send a draft to your supervisor a few days before a meeting. This allows your supervisor to read the draft and consider the feedback. Asking your supervisor to do this at the meeting is wasting your time, as the supervisor will probably not be able to read the draft and give immediate, detailed feedback. To keep the momentum going, it is helpful to record your meetings with your supervisor, identifying what the meeting was about and what you have agreed you will do next, as well as another date for a meeting.

Most students work best when given a deadline, so keeping a 'log' will help you pace yourself: it is helpful to know that by a certain time you have agreed to have completed something. Most students have the best intentions but somehow 'life' gets in the way and, without that deadline, it is easy to put things off. However, few students like to cancel meetings with their supervisor and, further, many would feel embarrassed coming to the meeting without anything prepared. It could be that your institution has its own way of recording tutorials or meetings with supervisors. If not, consider the pro forma below.

	Research log
Student	
Supervisor	
Research topic	
Progress to date	
Issues raised	
Actions/recommendations	
Date of next meeting	
Signed: 　Student 　Supervisor 　Date	

Experience shows that students achieving the highest marks for their research projects or dissertations are the ones who have worked closely with their supervisors, while those who work totally independently, if they complete at all, are awarded a much lower mark, often not quite meeting all the criteria.

C H A P T E R   S U M M A R Y

In this chapter we have examined what research actually is and have explained some different approaches to research, including positivism and interpretivism. We have given some guidance on how to select a research topic and then how to conduct a literature review. Methods of data collection and analysis were then described and we discussed some ethical considerations. Finally, we examined the role of the supervisor in your research project or dissertation.

Answers to tasks

Finding out about community support officers (page 153)

The first subject may be best researched by choosing an interpretive methodology. To find out about the experiences of community support officers it would be helpful to get their opinions and ideas. To collect the data you can conduct individual or focus group interviews. Of course, you cannot make any generalisations from this type of research; you can only find out about the community support officers on that particular estate. Experiences may be different elsewhere (although they may be similar).

The second subject would benefit from a positivist methodology. You can compare figures on anti-social behaviour before the introduction of community support officers to those after their introduction. However, you need to consider the sample and variables. Perhaps figures have fallen anyway, so maybe a drop is not a result of the community support officers (perhaps the person committing the most offences has moved away or is now in prison). If figures have risen, they may have risen even more without the community support officers. It may be wrong to conclude that figures have risen because of community support officers, suggesting that you would be better off without them.

REFERENCES

Burton, N, Brundrett, M and Jones, M (2008) *Doing your Education Research Project*. London: Sage.

Currie, D (2005) *Developing and Applying Study Skills*. London: CIPD.

Haralambos, M and Holborn, M (1995) *Sociology, Themes and Perspectives*, 4th edition. London: Collins Educational.

Koshy, V (2005) *Action Research for Improving Practice*. London: Sage.

Punch, K (2009) *Introduction to Research Methods in Education*. London: Sage.

Sharp, J (2009) *Success with Your Education Research Project*. Exeter: Learning Matters.

Swetnam, D (2000) *Writing your Dissertation*, 3rd edition. Oxford: How To Books.

www.homeoffice.gov.uk/rds/ (Home Office's Research Development Statistics page, which contains research and statistics publications relevant to crime, policing, etc.)

10 Writing your dissertation

Introduction

You have completed your research, drafted a literature review, justified your chosen methodology and methods of data collection, and analysed your data. All that remains to do is to put it together, usually in the form of a dissertation. As stated in Chapter 9, the dissertation is just as important as the research activity itself, as it ensures that the use of research results is maximised and that they are disseminated in an appropriate manner. The dissertation is a formal, extended piece of writing, not just reproducing information that is available elsewhere, but something new that adds to the body of knowledge. It is generally presented using a particular structure and a certain style.

This chapter discusses how to plan for the writing process and offers a commonly used structure and style for dissertations. Next, it focuses on punctuation, grammar and spelling, with some examples of common mistakes. Finally, the chapter makes some suggestions as to the overall presentation of a dissertation and offers a checklist for you to compare your dissertation against.

In general

Although it almost goes without saying, the first thing you need to do is check your institution's protocol: what are the expectations? For instance, what is the word count for the dissertation (usually 10,000 upwards) and does this include quotes or not? Some universities allow the word count to be 10 per cent under or over, while others are far stricter. Is there a certain format to which the dissertation is expected to conform, certain rules you should follow, or particular documents you should use? Further, make sure you find out the final submission date for your dissertation and the procedure for submission. For instance, should it be handed in to your supervisor, the administration office, the exams office, or the LRC, and will you be given a receipt?

Although you may not want to consider not completing, there could be circumstances, such as ill health, that interrupt the work. Therefore, find out what happens if you cannot make the submission date: are you allowed an extension for a few days; is there an 'extenuating circumstances' procedure? How long do you have to complete the dissertation? It alleviates stress and anxiety if you know such things beforehand, even if you do not plan to have to make use of these regulations.

Planning the writing process

Getting started is probably one of the most difficult things to do: when would be a good time? It is easy to put it off, thinking that you haven't done enough reading or analysis yet; in other words, it's easy to procrastinate. However, it is best to start drafting parts of the dissertation as soon as possible. Do not postpone the writing until you have finished the whole project, but draft each section as you work on it, so that the writing progresses as the project progresses. The methodology chapter, for instance, can probably be written quite early on. As it is likely that you had to write a proposal for the research, outlining a methodology, you can revisit this part of the proposal and build on it. Also, start your literature review as soon as possible. The reading around the subject started before you did anything else, so draft it up. Remember, it is always easier to edit, develop and improve a draft than start from a blank piece of paper. Share your drafts with your supervisor for feedback, as this allows your supervisor, and you, to monitor progress, and gives you the opportunity to fine-tune your writing where necessary.

Writing a dissertation can be a strange process. Normally, you would expect to start writing at the beginning of something and finish that part before you start the next. When writing a dissertation you probably work on several chapters at the same time, making slow progress in each and going back to parts you thought you had completed but now feel you can improve or want to change; this may impact on other parts, which now also need revisiting. You have noticed that the first part of the dissertation, the abstract, is written last. Even the introduction, although you may have started with an outline, probably gets rewritten at the end, making sure it ties in with the rest of the dissertation and the conclusions.

To be able to do this and stay sane, it is helpful to draw out a plan, setting yourself interim deadlines (pre-arranged meetings with your supervisor can act as such). Be realistic in your planning; do not aim for the impossible, as you will not be able to keep to your plan and this will only lead to you feeling demotivated. The process may be easier if you write regularly, having certain slots in the day or week during which you write, without being distracted. This then becomes a routine and other people around you know not to disturb you.

It may be helpful to ask your supervisor if you can have a look at a completed dissertation, to get some idea of what you are aiming for. Finally, keep the momentum going – a finished dissertation is something to be proud of. Look ahead and see yourself receiving your degree.

Planning the writing

- Begin early, do not wait until the final submission date is in sight.

- Write regularly, creating a routine.

- Set yourself realistic interim deadlines.

- Set a word count for each chapter, subdividing these into smaller parts, thus making the overall word count not so daunting but achievable.

- Stop writing at a point from which it is easy to resume.

- Make regular appointments with your supervisor.

- Submit drafts.

- Rework drafts.

- Rework drafts again.

- Stay focused.

Structure

The structure is one of the first things to consider. The usual convention is to divide the dissertation into the following sections; however, there may be occasions where, for example, there is a separate chapter on 'data analysis and discussion'. Therefore, the structure here is only a guideline and you should check with your supervisor what the convention is at your institution.

- Title page

- Acknowledgements

- Abstract

- List of contents

- Introduction (Chapter 1)

- Literature review (Chapter 2)

- Methodology/research design (Chapter 3)

- Data presentation and analysis (Chapter 4)

- Conclusions and recommendations (Chapter 5)

- References

- Appendices

Title page

Some institutions supply their own format. If not, a title page should at least include:

- the title of the research project, which should be brief and to the point; you may include a subtitle if that clarifies the study;

- your own name;

- the qualification for which the dissertation is submitted; the usual phrase is: 'submitted in partial fulfilment of the requirements of the award of . . .';

- the name of the institution;

- the month and year of submission.

An example of a title page is shown in the box below.

An investigation into the roots of youth crime
A case study

Julia Thomas

Submitted in partial fulfilment of the requirements for the degree of
Bachelor of Science in Crime and Criminology

University of Portsmouth

July 2009

Acknowledgements

Some students wish to acknowledge the support they have been given during the research process. This can be either from supervisors or tutors, or any other people or organisations that have made a significant contribution. Sharp (2009, p119) warns though that 'this is not the place to thank your parents for bringing you into the world and helping you to become the person you are or to thank your pets for their patience and undivided attention'.

Abstract

Whenever you submit a conference paper, research paper or dissertation, you will have to write an abstract. An abstract must be short, usually 200–250 words, giving a summary of your research. Abstracts that exceed the maximum word limit are often rejected because they cannot be used for databases, summaries of conferences, etc. As you have found from your literature search, the abstract is often the first contact you make with a piece of research. Therefore, it has to capture the interest of the reader, giving all the keywords, the methodology used, the main findings and conclusions. Writing an abstract can be a challenge. Consider the following steps.

- Read the dissertation again, specifically the purpose, methods, results and conclusion.

- Write a draft of the abstract, summarising the information (this does not mean copying sentences from the dissertation but rephrasing it, picking out the most important elements).

- Read the abstract again to check that it summarises your report. Drop unnecessary information; keep it succinct.

PRACTICAL TASK

Evaluate the following two abstracts, published in The British Journal of Criminology. *Do they give you all the information you need?*

Abstract 1: Gadd, D (2009) Aggravating racism and elusive motivation

> *Since the implementation of the 1998 Crime and Disorder Act, courts in England and Wales have seen an increase in the number of racially aggravated charges brought before them. However, the extent to which racism is central, rather than ancillary to, the offences prosecuted under this law remains contested, both in individual legal cases and in criminological writing about hate and bias-motivated crime. Using the narrative accounts of one man convicted of perpetrating a racially aggravated assault, this article outlines how important it is to engage with the complexity of motivation as it is perceived by offenders and the necessity of developing analytic approaches capable of transcending what offenders say about their attitudes to race.*

PRACTICAL TASK *continued*

Abstract 2: Charman, C and Savage, SP (2009) Mothers for justice? Gender and campaigns against miscarriages of justice

> *Miscarriages of justice are often only exposed through the extra-judicial activities of parties determined to fight for a particular cause, involving those closest to victims of miscarriages of justice. This paper examines the role of women, and particularly of mothers, in such justice campaigns and the extent to which there is a gendered dimension to campaigns against injustice. Based on interviews with those closely associated with justice campaigns, the paper argues that women tend to occupy a special, powerful place in campaigns against miscarriages of justice, one interwoven with familial relationships. The paper proceeds to relate this 'special' place to differential processes of grieving and the dynamics of women's engagement with protest and campaigning more generally.*

List of contents

List all the sections of your dissertation with the page number where they can be found. Check and double-check this for accuracy. Subheadings may also be added.

Page numbering usually starts from the introduction (title page, abstract, acknowledgements and contents are not numbered).

Introduction (Chapter 1)

The introduction provides the context of the study. You need to explain the reasons for undertaking the study and what you hope to achieve. This is where you introduce your research question, hypothesis or topic of research. Introductions are important, as they set the scene and explain where and when the research takes place, and who or what is being researched. You may look at trends or government policy, highlighting the gap in the current body of knowledge, which your study tries to fill. As stated by Koshy (2005), this chapter also provides a guide for the reader about what to expect in each chapter.

Literature review (Chapter 2)

This is a comprehensive review of the literature relating to your topic. You have to demonstrate that you are 'familiar with the field surrounding your chosen topic' (Sharp, 2009, p121). Draw from credible sources and remember to review the literature critically rather than offering a descriptive 'shopping list' of what you have read.

Methodology/research design (Chapter 3)

Within this chapter you describe and justify the structure of the research procedures and the methods you have adopted. You need to give an account of the strengths and limitations of your research tools and comment on the validity, reliability and general-isability of the research. You need to justify the population and sample (why were the participants selected) and also the locality (why did the research take place there). Finally, you need to consider the ethical issues that may have arisen and how you have dealt with these.

Data presentation and analysis (Chapter 4)

What did you find out? Present the data in a summarised version. It may be helpful to include tables, graphs and other illustrations, but don't do this for the sake of it (see Chapter 9). This section forms the heart of your research, as this is where you argue your case based on your findings. You may have to be ruthless, cutting out data that do not add to your argument. Although it may seem a waste of good data, there is no point giving information that is not relevant as it only clutters the argument. Further, as noted by Sharp (2009), finish this chapter by explaining to the reader how your findings fit in with literature you have reviewed.

Conclusions and recommendations (Chapter 5)

In this chapter of your dissertation you summarise the research, stating the key findings. Starting from the research question, guide the reader once more through the research process. Conclusions drawn from the findings should be consistent and logical, and linked to the initially stated objectives for the research. Do your findings reflect what other research has shown; are there contradictions? Make sure you don't make generalisations beyond the boundaries of the research. It is easy to make wide claims as you're probably enthusiastic and pleased with the results. Further, careful consideration needs to be given to the implications of the research or the impact on practice, so keep them realistic – are the recommendations practical? Finally, be careful not to introduce new information in this section; it may be tempting to throw in a final opinion or interesting quote, but this is not the place. Bell (2005) points out that readers who just want a quick look at the research will read the abstract, maybe the introduction and most likely the summary and conclusions. The final chapter should, therefore, be succinct and clearly expressed, so that the reader can understand what research has been conducted, and it should logically lead to conclusions that have been drawn from the evidence.

References

A full reference should be given for each publication, journal, internet site or other source that you have cited or referred to in the entire dissertation (this means material used for the literature review as well as literature on, for instance, research design). Most institutions use the Harvard method of referencing, listing all source materials in alphabetical order (by author). Some institutions also require a 'bibliography'; this lists all sources used although not necessarily cited or referred to. Referencing needs to be accurate to avoid accusations of plagiarism.

Appendices

Blank copies of research tools such as questionnaires, interview schedules, consent forms and participant information sheets can be filed in the appendices. Unless directed otherwise, do not include completed questionnaires or documents.

Writing style

After the structure of the dissertation, consider the writing style. According to Currie (2005, p125): 'Academic writing has to be clear, concise, grammatically correct and objective.' Arguably, the credibility of your report may suffer because of poor expression. Be aware that, if there are a number of grammatical or spelling errors in your work, there may be doubt as to your competence in other areas as well. If you do not write clearly, it may be implied that you do not think clearly either. Therefore, if you are aware that your grammar or spelling are not always accurate, do something about it.

The least you can do, and that is good practice anyway, is to ask someone else to read your work. If you need more support than that, consider making an appointment with your institution's learning support or learning skills department. They can offer individual support and guidance, addressing whatever learning needs you may have, such as spelling, structure or organisation of the work. Dyslexic learners may apply for software packages, such as voice-recognition packages, that can help them in writing up the dissertation.

Next, this chapter discusses appropriate writing styles and offers advice on punctuation, grammar and spelling, identifying some common errors.

Punctuation, grammar and spelling

First, be concise in your writing. This means 'getting as much information as you can in the smallest possible number of words without losing any of the context, integrity or meaning of what you are trying to say' (Currie, 2005, p126). Therefore, avoid the use of long sentences and long paragraphs. They may lead to confusion and boredom. Further, avoid writing in a chatty style, using clichés, colloquialisms or popular sayings; they may be appropriate for the local paper but not for your dissertation. This includes commonly used abbreviations: 'don't' should be written as 'do not'; 'isn't' as 'is not'. Acronyms, on the other hand, should be written out in full only the first time they are used. For instance, the National Police Improvement Agency (NPIA) can from now onwards be referred to as the NPIA.

Second, keep your writing as objective and dispassionate as possible. Don't be tempted to write in an opinionated, emotional style because you feel strongly about something. Keep the report balanced; this is not the platform for a rant or soapbox. Avoid using 'I believe' or 'I think' as, at this point, what you think is irrelevant. The use of 'we', on the other hand, sounds pretentious and should also be avoided.

Third, consider whether to use the 'active' or 'passive' voice and also the tense of your writing. The active voice uses the first person, or 'I'. For instance: 'I conducted semi-structured interviews.' This can get a bit tedious: I did this, and then I did that, I, I, I. A more general academic approach is to use the detached, passive voice. This voice uses the third person, for example: 'Data were collected by using semi-structured interviews.' The tense refers to the future, present or past. When writing a proposal for a research project, you probably write in the future tense: 'Data will be collected by using semi-structured interviews', as this is what you are planning to do at some point. After conducting the research, when you are writing it up, it is best to use the past tense. So, unless directed otherwise by your institution, the convention is to write in the third person, passive voice and past tense.

Finally, write correctly. As advised by Sharp (2009, p128), 'aim for nothing short of the highest standard of grammar, spelling and punctuation and do not rely solely on the spelling and grammar checkers on your computer'.

Punctuation

The most common mistake in punctuation is the incorrect use of the **apostrophe**. Apostrophes are used to show possession of something (not to indicate a plural!):

- the police officer's uniform;
- the judge's decision.

If the word is plural and already ends in 's', add an apostrophe after the 's':

- five officers' uniforms.

If you use someone's name, add 's even if the name ends with an 's':

- Charles's uniform.

The same applies when a noun ends in 'ss':

- The boss's uniform.

You can also use an apostrophe to show where a letter has been left out, for example:

- it's (it is);
- don't (do not).

However, in your dissertation you are advised to avoid these abbreviations.

Be precise when using **commas**, as putting the comma in the wrong place can alter the meaning of the sentence. Consider the following examples (from Malthouse and Roffey-Barentsen, 2009).

- I can't think how to go about it your way.
- I can't think how to, go about it your way.
- I can't, think how to go about it your way.

Commas are also used to list items within a sentence. For instance: methods for data collection included semi-structured interviews, observations, questionnaires and documents.

The main use of a **colon** is to introduce a list or series, or a quotation, for example:

- The following methods of data collection were employed: semi-structured interviews, observations, questionnaires and documents.

- According to Sharp (2009, p128): 'spelling and grammar checkers on your computer are by no means foolproof'.

A **semi-colon** can be used instead of a full stop to separate two statements or to combine two ideas into one sentence:

- Interviews are a valid method of data collection; triangulation enhances reliability.

It is also used in contrasting statements:

- Transcribing interviews is time consuming; collating quantitative data is not.

Grammar

Grammar covers sentence structure, word order, tense and agreement.

According to Swetnam (2000, p89), a very common error in students' work is failure to get the subject of a sentence to agree with the verb, for example:

The group of participants, who seemed to have much to contribute, were not prepared to be interviewed.

'The group of participants' is the subject of the sentence and is singular. Therefore 'were' should be changed to 'was'.

Further, carefully consider the word order in your sentence, as this can affect the meaning; make sure your sentence says what you mean it to say:

Three Australian nationals, just released from prison in Sierra Leone, gave a horrifying account of torture and appalling conditions that they had suffered when they arrived at Sydney Airport.

This sentence implies that the torture occurred at Sydney Airport. Is that what you meant to report? Another way of ordering the information is:

When they arrived at Sydney Airport, three Australian nationals, just released from prison in Sierra Leone, gave horrifying accounts of the torture and appalling conditions they had suffered.

Again, careful proof-reading should address any ambiguities and inaccuracies.

Spelling

Always check your spelling. Some words are regularly misspelt, and they will be highlighted by your computer; other words are wrong in that context. They are homophones (sound the same but are spelled differently and have different meanings); they will not be identified by a computer, as their spelling is correct.

PRACTICAL TASK

Identify the 20 incorrectly used homophones in the following passage.

> *As a Police Community Support Officer, I can't weight two see the fare. It is the principle event of the year and it brings the best out of the local people. I hope it is as good as last year. I was off duty at the time and remember won ride heard me so much it gave me a pane in my side witch lasted up too a weak. I will sea if the bumper cars are in the same plaice, it would be nice to meat up their again. Although eye remember they maid me feel a little sick. I think the fair is grate. What do yew think, am I rite or knot?*

(adapted from Malthouse and Roffey-Barentsen, 2009, p21)

(The answers are given at the end of the chapter.)

In general, the words most frequently confused are:

- principle (origin or general law) and principal (main or head):

  'the principles of the Principal were questionable';

- advice (noun) and advise (verb):

  'we advise you to accept the advice';

- practice (noun) and practise (verb):

  'practising these exercises will help to improve your practice';

- to, too and two:

  'the two words that are confused all too often cause me to wince';

- there, their and they're:

  'there are always people in the park who think they're there for their dog's exercise'.

Swetnam (2000, p89) offers the following advice: 'If you know you habitually confuse "there" and "their" try fitting "here" into the same space: if it makes some sort of sense, "there" is the one to use.'

Words that are commonly misspelt include:

accommodate, complementary/complimentary, necessary, questionnaire, liaison, management, qualitative, quantitative, analysis, committee, commitment, committed, dependent/dependant, consensus, conscience, conscientious, conscious, occasionally, parallel, variable, separate, changeable, column, privilege, definite.

'sion' and 'tion'

Words ending in sion and tion are usually nouns that are formed from verbs.

Nouns ending in sion are formed from verbs ending in:

Examples	Verb	Noun ('sion')
nd	expand	expansion
de	provide	provision
ss	discuss	discussion
mit	omit	omission
pel	propel	propulsion
vert	divert	diversion.

Nouns ending in tion are formed from verbs ending in:

Examples	Verb	Noun ('tion')
ct	act	action
te	create	creation
ise	organise	organisation
ose	suppose	supposition
erve	reserve	reservation.

When the sound is 'shun' never write 'sh' except for fashion and cushion. Nearly all the others end with 'tion'.

'ant' and 'ent'

'Ant' and 'ent' words are among the most commonly misspelt words. There is no rule for the types of words that end in 'ant' and 'ent'. But there is a rule which observes that words ending in 'ance' will always be formed from words that end in 'ant', in the same way that words ending in 'ence' come from 'ent' words, for example:

predominant   predominance

different   difference.

Y

When you add something to a word that ends in a 'y', change the 'y' to an 'i', except when you add 'ing':

	Adding 'ies'	Adding 'ied'	Adding 'ing'
carry	carries	carried	carrying
hurry	hurries	hurried	hurrying
supply	supplies	supplied	supplying.

'able' and 'ible'

This is another problematic ending to a word. The rule is: If the part of the word before the ending is complete, the end will be 'able':

know	knowable
read	readable.

If the part of the word before the ending is not complete, the end will be 'ible':

permiss	permissible
ed	edible.

'all', 'full' and 'till'

When 'all', 'full' and 'till' are joined to a word, or part of a word, they drop an 'l', for example: also, hopeful, until, always, altogether, almost.

'er' and 'or'

Both 'er' and 'or' endings are found in words that describe what people do, for example: banker, gaoler, tailor, director.

In words that describe what things do, 'or' is the more common ending, for example: detonator, refrigerator, incubator. There are exceptions, though, most notably computer.

'ei' and 'ie'

You may be familiar with the phrase, 'i before e, except after c whenever it rhymes with me'. This is a useful rule to remember (but beware of exceptions, such as the word 'seize'):

'i' before 'e'	**except after c**
chief	ceiling
field	deceive
yield	receive
shield	deceit
priest	conceive.

Plurals

Plurals often cause students to make mistakes. There are different types of plurals:

- regular plurals;
- mutated plurals;
- nouns that are the same when plural;
- nouns that are never singular.

Regular plurals

To make a word a plural you add an 's' to it (not an apostrophe then an 's'!), for example: dog**s**, sofa**s**, shoe**s**, book**s**.

Nouns that end in a hissing sound (sibilant) need 'es' to be added to them when they are plural, unless they already end in an 'e', for example: bus**es**, class**es**, wish**es**, siz**es**.

If there is a vowel (a, e, i, o, u) before the last 'y' in a word, add an 's' to make the word plural, for example: key – key**s**; bay – bay**s**.

However, if there is a consonant (every letter that is not a vowel) before the 'y', the 'y' gets changed to an 'i' and then you add 'es', for example: berry – ber**ries**; century – centu**ries**.

Mutated plurals

Some words change internally when they become plurals, and these are known as mutated plurals, for example:

child	children
die	dice
foot	feet
man	men
penny	pence
tooth	teeth
woman	women.

Nouns that are the same when plural

A few words remain in the same form whether they are singular or plural:

aircraft

deer

forceps

salmon

sheep.

Nouns that are never singular

These nouns are never singular:

binoculars	pincers
eaves	pliers
measles	scissors
news	spectacles
pants	trousers.

Be aware that the spell-checker on your computer may use an American dictionary, using 'behavior' rather than the English 'behaviour', 'organize' rather than 'organise', etc. Some markers may have a preference for the English language; however, whichever dictionary you use, be consistent in your spelling.

Overall presentation

Finally, make sure your hard work looks good too. This does not necessarily mean illustrating it with pretty flowers and cute pictures: keep your dissertation professional and treat it as an official document. Your institution may have a preference with regard to fonts, margins or line-spacing. There may be a requirement for your dissertation to be bound professionally. If so, ask your supervisor to recommend a suitable bookbinder, experienced in binding dissertations for the institution. Below are some general suggestions on the presentation of your dissertation.

- Use A4 size paper, writing on one side only.

- Margins: top and right-hand margin 20 mm; left-hand margin (spine) 40 mm; bottom margin 40 mm.

- Use 12-point typeface, such as Arial or Times New Roman, and 1.5 line spacing.

- Use 14-point bold for the section titles, then reduce to 12-point bold for sub-headings.

- Start each chapter on a new page, with a top margin of 40 mm.

- Start page numbering on first page of the Introduction, using Arabic numerals, 20 mm from the bottom of the page, usually centred between the margin lines. Change the page number default setting to your chosen text font.

- Numbers 1 to 9 should be written in full; beyond nine you can use figures. Numbers at the start of a sentence should always be written in full.

- When using tables, charts or other illustrations, avoid bold colours; label all axes where necessary, and give a title.

- Collate appendices in the same order as you refer to them in the text.

- Avoid plastic wallets for individual pages.

- Bind the dissertation in an attractive and robust cover.

Dissertation checklist

Before you bind your work formally, take this one last chance to check everything is there and in its right place. It may be useful to ask a 'critical friend' to help you with this process, as it is easy to miss things if you have been working with them this closely for so long. It may help to use the checklist below.

Abstract	Is abstract clear and within word limit?	✓
Introduction	Is the purpose for the research clear?	
	Is the context clear?	
Literature review	Does literature underpin theory?	
	Is there a range of literature sources?	
	Are quotes relevant?	
	Is literature critically reviewed?	
Methodology	Is the methodology justified?	
	Is there a justification for the location and participants?	
	Are strengths and limitations of methods of data collection discussed?	
	Is research valid, reliable; can you generalise from the research?	
	Are ethical considerations discussed?	
Data presentation and analysis	Is data presentation clear?	
	Is interpretation of data convincing?	
	Are tables and figures named and numbered?	
Conclusions and recommendations	Do the conclusions follow logically from the presented data?	
	Is there a clear link with the objectives of the research?	
	Are recommendations practical?	
Structure and presentation	Are chapters balanced and well structured?	
	Have you checked punctuation, grammar and spelling?	
	Are all references accurate?	
	Do page numbers match contents list?	

C H A P T E R   S U M M A R Y

In this chapter we have described how to plan the writing process and how to structure your dissertation. The importance of adopting an appropriate writing style was stressed and we then went on to detail some of the common mistakes made in punctuation, grammar and spelling. Finally, we gave some general suggestions for the presentation of a dissertation and offered a dissertation checklist.

Answers to tasks

Homophones (page 180)

Weight – wait; two – to; fare – fair; principle – principal; won – one; heard – hurt; pane – pain; witch – which; too – to; weak – week; sea – see; plaice – place; meat – meet; their – there; eye – I; maid – made; grate – great; yew – you; rite – right; knot – not.

Bell, J (2005) *Doing Your Research Project*, 4th edition. Buckingham: Open University Press.

Charman, C and Savage, SP (2009) Mothers for Justice? Gender and campaigns against miscarriages of justice. *The British Journal of Criminology*, 49: 900–15.

Currie, D (2005) *Developing and Applying Study Skills*. London: CIPD.

Gadd, D (2009) Aggravating racism and elusive motivation. *The British Journal of Criminology*, 49: 755–71.

Koshy, V (2005) *Action Research for Improving Practice*. London: Sage.

Malthouse, R and Roffey-Barentsen, J (2009) *Written Exercises for the Police Recruit Assessment Process*. Exeter: Learning Matters.

Sharp, J (2009) *Success with Your Education Research Project*. Exeter: Learning Matters.

Swetnam, D (2000) *Writing your dissertation*, 3rd edition. Oxford: How To Books.

Levin, P (2005) *Excellent Dissertations*. Maidenhead: Open University Press.

Appendix:
keyboard shortcuts

Table A.1 Some keyboard shortcuts for Word 2002, Word 2003, and Word 2007

Command name	Shortcut keys	Command name	Shortcut keys
All Caps	CTRL+SHIFT+A	Copy Text	SHIFT+F2
Annotation	ALT+CTRL+M	Create Auto Text	ALT+F3
App Maximise	ALT+F10	Customise Add Menu	ALT+CTRL+=
App Restore	ALT+F5	Customise Keyboard	ALT+CTRL+
Apply Heading1	ALT+CTRL+1		NUM +
Apply Heading2	ALT+CTRL+2	Customise Remove	ALT+CTRL+-
Apply Heading3	ALT+CTRL+3	Menu	
Apply List Bullet	CTRL+SHIFT+L	Cut	CTRL+X or
Auto Format	ALT+CTRL+K		SHIFT+DELETE
Auto Text	F3 or ALT+CTRL+V	Date Field	ALT+SHIFT+D
Bold	CTRL+B or CTRL+	Delete Back Word	CTRL+
	SHIFT+B		BACKSPACE
Bookmark	CTRL+SHIFT+F5	Delete Word	CTRL+DELETE
Browse Next	CTRL+PAGE DOWN	Dictionary	ALT+SHIFT+F7
Browse Previous	CTRL+PAGE UP	Do Field Click	ALT+SHIFT+F9
Browse Sel	ALT+CTRL+HOME	Doc Close	CTRL+W or
Cancel	ESC		CTRL+F4
Centre Para	CTRL+E	Doc Maximise	CTRL+F10
Change Case	SHIFT+F3	Doc Move	CTRL+F7
Char Left	LEFT	Doc Restore	CTRL+F5
Char Left Extend	SHIFT+LEFT	Doc Size	CTRL+F8
Char Right	RIGHT	Doc Split	ALT+CTRL+S
Char Right Extend	SHIFT+RIGHT	Double Underline	CTRL+SHIFT+D
Clear	DELETE	End of Column	ALT+PAGE DOWN
Close or Exit	ALT+F4	End of Column	ALT+SHIFT+
Close Pane	ALT+SHIFT+C		PAGE DOWN
Column Break	CTRL+SHIFT+ENTER	End of Doc Extend	CTRL+SHIFT+
Column Select	CTRL+SHIFT+F8		END
Copy	CTRL+C or CTRL+INSERT	End of Document	CTRL+END
Copy Format	CTRL+SHIFT+C	End of Line	END

Command name	Shortcut keys	Command name	Shortcut keys
End of Line Extend	SHIFT+END	Menu Mode	F10
End of Row	ALT+END	Merge Field	ALT+SHIFT+F
End of Row	ALT+SHIFT+END	Microsoft Script	ALT+SHIFT+F11
End of Window	ALT+CTRL+PAGE DOWN	Editor	
End of Window	ALT+CTRL+SHIFT+	Microsoft System Info	ALT+CTRL+F1
Extend	PAGE DOWN	Move Text	F2
Endnote Now	ALT+CTRL+D	New	CTRL+N
Extend Selection	F8	Next Cell	TAB
Field Chars	CTRL+F9	Next Field	F11 or ALT+F1
Field Codes	ALT+F9	Next Misspelling	ALT+F7
Find	CTRL+F	Next Object	ALT+DOWN
Font	CTRL+D or	Next Window	CTRL+F6 or
	CTRL+SHIFT+F		ALT+F6
Font Size Select	CTRL+SHIFT+P	Normal	ALT+CTRL+N
Footnote Now	ALT+CTRL+F	Normal Style	CTRL+SHIFT+N
Go Back	SHIFT+F5 or ALT+CTRL+Z		or ALT+
Go To	CTRL+G or F5		SHIFT+CLEAR
Grow Font	CTRL+SHIFT+		(NUM 5)
Grow Font One Point	CTRL+]	Open	CTRL+O or
Hanging Indent	CTRL+T		CTRL+F12 or
Header Footer Link	ALT+SHIFT+R		ALT+CTRL+F2
Help	F1	Open or Close Up	CTRL+0
Hidden	CTRL+SHIFT+H	Para	
Hyperlink	CTRL+K	Other Pane	F6 or SHIFT+F6
Indent	CTRL+M	Outline	ALT+CTRL+O
Italic	CTRL+I or CTRL+SHIFT+I	Outline Collapse	ALT+SHIFT+- or
Justify Para	CTRL+J		ALT+SHIFT+
Left Para	CTRL+L		NUM-
Line Down	DOWN	Outline Demote	ALT+SHIFT+
Line Down Extend	SHIFT+DOWN		RIGHT
Line Up	UP	Outline Expand	ALT+SHIFT+=
Line Up Extend	SHIFT+UP	Outline Expand	ALT+SHIFT+
List Num Field	ALT+CTRL+L		NUM+
Lock Fields	CTRL+3 or CTRL+F11	Outline Move Down	ALT+SHIFT+
Macro	ALT+F8		DOWN
Mail Merge Check	ALT+SHIFT+K	Outline Move Up	ALT+SHIFT+UP
Mail Merge Edit	ALT+SHIFT+E	Outline Promote	ALT+SHIFT+
Data Source			LEFT
Mail Merge to Doc	ALT+SHIFT+N	Outline Show	ALT+SHIFT+L
Mail Merge to Printer	ALT+SHIFT+M	First Line	
Mark Citation	ALT+SHIFT+I	Overtype	INSERT
Mark Index Entry	ALT+SHIFT+X	Page	ALT+CTRL+P
Mark Table of Contents	ALT+SHIFT+O	Page Break	CTRL+ENTER
Entry		Page Down	PAGE DOWN

Command name	Shortcut keys	Command name	Shortcut keys
Page Down Extend	SHIFT+PAGE DOWN	Show Heading1	ALT+SHIFT+1
Page Field	ALT+SHIFT+P	Show Heading2	ALT+SHIFT+2
Page Up	PAGE UP	Show Heading3	ALT+SHIFT+3
Page Up Extend	SHIFT+PAGE UP	Show Heading4	ALT+SHIFT+4
Para Down	CTRL+DOWN	Show Heading5	ALT+SHIFT+5
Para Down Extend	CTRL+SHIFT+DOWN	Show Heading6	ALT+SHIFT+6
Para Up	CTRL+UP	Show Heading7	ALT+SHIFT+7
Para Up Extend	CTRL+SHIFT+UP	Show Heading8	ALT+SHIFT+8
Paste	CTRL+V or SHIFT+ INSERT	Show Heading9	ALT+SHIFT+9
		Shrink Font	CTRL+SHIFT+
Paste Format	CTRL+SHIFT+V	Shrink Font One Point	CTRL+[
Prev Cell	SHIFT+TAB		
Prev Field	SHIFT+F11 or ALT+SHIFT+F1	Small Caps	CTRL+SHIFT+K
		Space Para1	CTRL+1
Prev Object	ALT+UP	Space Para2	CTRL+2
Prev Window	CTRL+SHIFT+F6 or ALT+SHIFT+F6	Spike	CTRL+SHIFT+F3 or CTRL+F3
Print	CTRL+P or CTRL+ SHIFT+F12	Start of Column	ALT+PAGE UP
		Start of Column	ALT+SHIFT+ PAGE UP
Print Preview	CTRL+F2 or ALT+CTRL+I	Start of Doc Extend	CTRL+SHIFT+ HOME
Proofing	F7		
Redo	ALT+SHIFT+ BACKSPACE	Start of Document	CTRL+HOME
		Start of Line	HOME
Redo or Repeat	CTRL+Y or F4 or ALT+ ENTER	Start of Line Extend	SHIFT+HOME
		Start of Row	ALT+HOME
Repeat Find	SHIFT+F4 or ALT+CTRL+Y	Start of Row	ALT+SHIFT+ HOME
Replace	CTRL+H	Start of Window	ALT+CTRL+ PAGE UP
Reset Char	CTRL+SPACE or CTRL+SHIFT+Z		
		Start of Window Extend	ALT+CTRL+ SHIFT+PAGE UP
Reset Para	CTRL+Q		
Revision Marks Toggle	CTRL+SHIFT+E	Style	CTRL+SHIFT+S
		Subscript	CTRL+=
Right Para	CTRL+R	Superscript	CTRL+SHIFT+=
Save	CTRL+S or SHIFT+F12 or ALT+SHIFT+F2	Symbol Font	CTRL+SHIFT+Q
		Thesaurus	SHIFT+F7
		Time Field	ALT+SHIFT+T
Save As	F12	Toggle Field Display	SHIFT+F9
Select All	CTRL+A or CTRL+ CLEAR (NUM 5) or CTRL+NUM 5	Toggle Master Subdocs	CTRL+\
Select Table	ALT+CLEAR (NUM 5)	Tool	SHIFT+F1
Show All	CTRL+SHIFT+8	Un Hang	CTRL+SHIFT+T
Show All Headings	ALT+SHIFT+A	Un Indent	CTRL+SHIFT+M

Command name	Shortcut keys	Command name	Shortcut keys
Underline	CTRL+U or CTRL+SHIFT+U	VBCode Web Go Back	ALT+F11 ALT+LEFT
Undo	CTRL+Z or ALT+BACKSPACE	Web Go Forward Word Left	ALT+RIGHT CTRL+LEFT
Unlink Fields	CTRL+6 or CTRL+SHIFT+F9	Word Left Extend	CTRL+SHIFT+ LEFT
Unlock Fields	CTRL+4 or CTRL+SHIFT+F11	Word Right Word Right Extend	CTRL+RIGHT CTRL+SHIFT+
Update Auto Format	ALT+CTRL+U		RIGHT
Update Fields	F9 or ALT+SHIFT+U	Word Underline	CTRL+SHIFT+W
Update Source	CTRL+SHIFT+F7		

Index